Structure & Speaking Practice
Dubai

NATIONAL GEOGRAPHIC
L E A R N I N G

Australia • Brazil • Mexico • Singapore • United Kingdom • United States

National Geographic Learning,
a Cengage Company

Structure & Speaking Practice, Dubai

Nancy Douglas and James R. Morgan

Publisher: Sherrise Roehr

Executive Editor: Laura LeDréan

Managing Editor: Jennifer Monaghan

Digital Implementation Manager,
Irene Boixareu

Senior Media Researcher: Leila Hishmeh

Director of Global Marketing: Ian Martin

Regional Sales and National Account
Manager: Andrew O'Shea

Content Project Manager: Ruth Moore

Senior Designer: Lisa Trager

Manufacturing Planner: Mary Beth
Hennebury

Composition: Lumina Datamatics

Student Edition: Structure & Speaking Practice, Dubai
ISBN-13: 978-0-357-13794-9

National Geographic Learning
20 Channel Center Street
Boston, MA 02210
USA

Locate your local office at **international.cengage.com/region**

Visit National Geographic Learning online at **ELTNGL.com**
Visit our corporate website at **www.cengage.com**

Printed in China
Print Number: 02   Print Year: 2019

Photo Credits

SCOPE & SEQUENCE

Unit / Lesson	Video	Vocabulary	Listening

UNIT 1 GOALS p. 2

LESSON A
Starting out

Young Entrepreneurs

Applying to college
apply, consider, compete, decide

Not your typical school
Listen for details
Summarize

LESSON B
After graduation

Life after graduation
do an internship, take time off, at some point

Plans for the future
Listen for gist
Listen for details

UNIT 2 STORYTELLING p. 16

LESSON A
What's the story about?

Star Wars Subway Car

TV Shows
made-up, characters, realistic, violent

Crowdsourcing
Infer information
Listen for details

LESSON B
Modern fairy tales

Modern fairy tales
discover, overcome, struggle

The moral of the story
Build background knowledge
Make predictions
Listen for main ideas
Listen for details
Summarize

UNIT 3 TECHNOLOGY p. 30

LESSON A
Then and now

Kids React to Old Computers

Describe new products
portable, affordable, dependable

Technology through the ages
Listen for the main idea
Listen for details
Note taking

LESSON B
Making life better

The Great Pacific Garbage Patch
locate, consume, restore, transform

New products to help people
Listen for gist
Listen for details
Listen to sequence events

UNIT 4 TELEPHONING p. 44

LESSON A
Using the telephone

A Conference Call in Real Life

Using the phone
call someone, answer the phone, get a text message

Talking about electronic communication
Make and check predictions
Infer information

LESSON B
Always connected

Phone etiquette
add, respond, turn down, ban

What are the speakers doing?
Listen for gist
Listen for details; Infer information

Expansion Activities p. 58

Grammar	Pronunciation	Speaking	Reading	Writing	Communication
Plans and decisions with *be going to* and *will* Predictions with *be going to* and *will*	Reduced form of *going to*	Responding to bad news / Offering to help	A different road to success Draw conclusions Infer meaning Scan for details Identify pros and cons	Write about your college experience	Asking and answering questions about future plans Making predictions about someone's future
The past continuous tense: statements / questions Adverbs of manner	Compound words	Keeping a story going	The Cinderella story Use background knowledge Identify main ideas Scan for details	Write an email about a previous event	Telling an unusual story Describe a scene from a picture
Used to Comparisons with *as... as*	*Used to*	Offering a counterargument	Robots to the rescue Make predictions Infer meaning Sequence events	Compare products	Describing life changes Designing and describing your own robot
Asking for permission Verb + infinitive vs. verb + gerund	Stress in clarification questions	Using the telephone	Phone-free on the road? Read for the gist Read for opinions Infer meaning Summarize and evaluate Exemplify	Describe your phone use	Giving and taking messages on the phone Stating and supporting your opinion

Language Summaries p. 66   Grammar Notes p. 68

1 GOALS

People work together at Google's European headquarters in Dublin, Ireland.

Look at the photo. Answer the questions.

1 What are some of the most well-known companies in your country?

2 Do you know anyone who works at these places?

3 Would you want to work at a place like the one in the photo?

UNIT GOALS

1 Describe how to apply to a school

2 Respond to bad news and offer to help

3 Talk about educational and work goals

4 Make predictions about the future

A *job fair* (also, *career fair*) is an event where job hunters can meet many possible employers in one place.

1 VIDEO Young Entrepreneurs

A Read the statistic from the video. What do you think the video is going to be about? Tell a partner.

Only 1 in 4 college graduates will graduate with a job.

B There are four people in the video. Read the items in the chart. Then watch the video. Check (✓) the answers.

	Jason Zima	John Campbell	Scott Gerber	Christy Tyler
is a senior at Babson College				
feels discouraged				
got a job while still in school				
majored in business	✓			
opened a shoe store				
started a photography business				
started several businesses				
teaches business classes				
went to a job fair	✓			

C Discuss the questions with a partner.

1. Look at your answers in **B**. Who do you think is going to be most successful? Why?

2. Are there job fairs in your country?

3. How do new college graduates find jobs? How hard is it?

2 VOCABULARY

Word Bank

apply → application

consider → consideration

compete → competition

decide → decision

observe → observation

recommend → recommendation

A Read the instructions for applying to college in the United States. Finish writing the incomplete words. Use the correct form of the words in the Word Bank.

- Look at different colleges' websites. (1.) _Con_____ these questions: Where is the school located? Does it offer your major? How big are the class sizes?

- Make a list of all the colleges that interest you.

- Top schools receive thousands of (2.) _app_____. There is a lot of (3.) _com_____ for few openings. Be realistic in your goals.

- Visit some of the schools on your list. Talk to students at the school. How do they like it?

- (4.) _Ob_____ some classes at the school. Are the classes interesting?

- Ask your high school teachers to write letters of (5.) _rec_____ for you.

- (6.) _De_____ which schools to (7.) _app_____ to. Your (8.) _app_____ should be sent no later than January.

- Most schools will give you their (9.) _de_____ by April. You choose your school in May and start in August or September.

  Good luck!

B 🕮 Review the steps in **A** with a partner. How is applying to college different in your country? How is it similar?

ℹ️ **Usage notes**
apply **to** a school, decide **to do** something, consider **doing** something, recommend **that** someone do something

C 🔗 Read the message Kento posted on an online forum. What is Kento's problem? What advice would you give him? Discuss in small groups.

I'm trying to choose a college. My parents want me to apply to Tokyo University. It's one of the best colleges in Japan, and it's very competitive. I'm not even sure I want to go to college right now. I need some advice because I can't decide what to do!

—Kento

Tokyo University

Kento should consider waiting a year. He doesn't have to apply to college right now.

But what about his parents' feelings? I recommend that he...

3 LISTENING

A You're going to hear an interview about a special school. How do you think Stratton Mountain School is special? Look at the profile below and guess the answers.

B 🔊 **Listen for details.** A student is going to talk about the school below. Listen and complete the profile. **Track 1**

STRATTON MOUNTAIN SCHOOL

Stratton Mountain School is a _____-year _____ school for students between _____ and _____ years old.

Where: Vermont, US

Students: Most are _____ or snowboarders. After graduation, some compete in the Winter _____.

A typical day at Stratton:

7:00 AM: _____

8:00 AM to _____:
Students are in _____.

12:30 to 5:00 PM:
Students have _____.

C 🔁 **Summarize.** Review the profile in **B**. Then cover your notes and answer the questions about Stratton with a partner.

1. Who goes to Stratton?   2. Why do they go there?   3. What is a typical day like?

D 🔊 Read the sentences below. Then listen. Choose the correct answer for each one.
Track 2

1. A *coed* school admits…
   a. boys only.
   b. girls only.
   c. both boys and girls.

2. A *dorm* is where students…
   a. live.
   b. train.
   c. study.

3. A school's *alumni* are…
   a. graduates of the school.
   b. students now at the school.
   c. teachers at the school.

E 🔁 Do you think Stratton is an interesting school? Why or why not? Discuss with a partner.

4 SPEAKING

A 🔊 🔄 Listen to the conversation. Then answer the questions with a partner. **Track 3**

1. Tom is unhappy about something. What?

2. How does Hans respond to Tom's bad news? Underline Hans's responses.

3. Do you think Hans is a good friend? Why or why not?

HANS: Hey, Tom. How's it going with the college applications?

TOM: Not so well. I didn't get into McGill University.

HANS: Oh no! I'm sorry to hear that.

TOM: Yeah, and McGill was my first choice.

HANS: You must be disappointed. Did you apply to any other schools?

TOM: Yes, three other ones.

HANS: And?

TOM: I don't know yet. I'm waiting to hear back from them.

HANS: Well, good luck.

TOM: Thanks.

HANS: And if you want to talk, just call me.

TOM: Thanks, Hans. I really appreciate it.

B 🔄 Practice the conversation with a partner.

SPEAKING STRATEGY

C 🔄 Do the role play below with a partner. Practice responding to bad news and offering to help. Use the Useful Expressions and the conversation in **A** to help you.

Useful Expressions	
Responding to bad news	**Offering to help**
(I'm) sorry to hear that. That's too bad. How disappointing. You must be disappointed.	If you want to talk, (just) call me. If there's anything I can do, (just) let me know.

Student A: You just received an exam back. You didn't fail the test, but your grade is much lower than expected.

Student B: Respond to Student A's news, and offer to help.

D 🔄 Switch roles and do the role play again.

5 GRAMMAR

A Turn to page 68. Complete the exercises. Then do **B–E** below.

Plans and Decisions with *be going to* and *will*			
	I'm / You're / He's / She's / We're / They're	(not)	**going to** go to Harvard.
Maybe	I / you / he / she / we / they	**will** **won't**	see a movie.

B 🔊 **Pronunciation: Reduced form of *going to.*** How do you pronounce *going to* in each sentence? Say the sentences aloud. Then listen and repeat. **Track 4**

1. I'm going to consider taking a year off.
2. We're going to visit all of them.
3. She's going to write a recommendation.
4. You're going to have a great time!

C Circle the best answer for each item.

1. A: What are your plans for tonight?
   B: I'll / I'm going to study.

2. A: We need your application by 5:00 PM today.
   B: I'll / I'm going to do it right now.

3. A: When's the competition tomorrow?
   B: It'll / It's going to start at 9:00 AM.

4. A: What will you / are you going to do on your campus visit?
   B: Observe some classes.

5. A: What are your plans for this afternoon?
   B: Maybe I'll / I'm going to do some homework.

6. A: Who's writing your letter of recommendation?
   B: I'll / I'm going to ask Mr. Stuart, my math teacher.

D Imagine you can go to any school in the world. Choose a school and complete the sentences.

1. I'll apply to _____ schools.
   (number)

2. I'll go to _____.
   (name of school)

3. I'll live at / in _____.
   (home / a dorm room / my own apartment)

4. I'll study _____.
   (name of major)

5. I'll graduate in _____ years.
   (number)

6. After graduation, I'll become _____.
   (*a / an* + job)

E 🔄 Ask questions to get your partner's answers to **D**. On a piece of paper, write six questions with *be going to* and the question words below. Take turns asking and answering the questions with a partner.

ℹ️ At the moment you are making a decision about the future, use *will*. Once you have made the decision, use *be going to.*

1. How many...?
2. Where...?
3. Where...?
4. What...?
5. When...?
6. What...?

6 COMMUNICATION

A 🔄 The two questions in the chart ask about someone's future plans. Read the answers. Then complete each question with *be going to*. Check answers with a partner.

| Yes / No questions | _____ study English this summer? | Yes, I am. / Maybe. / No, I'm not. |
| Wh- questions | What _____ do after graduation? | I'm going to take a trip. |

B Read the questions on the left side of the chart. In the *Me* column, check (✔) the activities you're planning to do in the future. Then add your own question.

Are you going to...	Me	Classmate's name	Wh- Question	Answer
graduate from high school or college soon?			When...?	
take a trip somewhere this summer?			Where...?	
go out this weekend?			Who...?	
study after class today?			What...?	
take a test in English (like the TOEFL) soon?			Which...?	
keep studying English after this class?			Where...?	
_____?				

C 🔶 Interview your classmates. For each question, find a different person who answers *yes*. Write the classmate's name in the chart above. Ask a *Wh-* question to get more details.

> Are you going to study after class today?

> Yes, I am.

> Where are you going to study?

> In the park.

D 🔶 Look at the answers you got above. Which one was the most interesting? Tell the class.

1 VOCABULARY

A The people below are college seniors or recent graduates. Take turns reading each opinion aloud with a partner.

"I want to <u>do an internship</u> this summer. **At some point** before then, I have to <u>create a résumé</u>." —Linh

"I'm going to <u>take time off</u> **in the near future**, maybe after graduation, and go on vacation." —Martina

"I'm working now, but **eventually**, I'd like to <u>go back to school</u> and get my PhD." —Roberto

"**Someday**, I'd like to <u>be my own boss</u>, but not yet. I have a lot to learn still." —Simon

Word Bank
Definite future time
after graduation
in a month
next year
this summer
Indefinite future time
soon
in a few days / weeks
in the near future
at some point
someday / eventually

B Look at the underlined expressions in **A**. Answer the questions. Then tell a partner.

Which person wants to…

1. return to school? _____

2. work somewhere and learn to do a job? _____

3. work for himself? _____

4. not work or study for a short time? _____

5. create a summary of her education and job experience? _____

C When do the people in **A** want to do these things? Do they give a definite future time or not? Tell a partner.

D Look again at the underlined expressions in **A**. Do you want to do any of these things? If yes, when? Use the future time expressions to tell a partner.

2 LISTENING

A 🔊 **Listen for gist.** You are going to hear three different conversations. In each, which sentence is true? Listen and circle the best answer. **Track 5**

1. a. She's going to graduate soon.

   b. She is applying to school.

   c. She just got accepted to a good school.

2. a. She's working on her résumé.

   b. She's going to be her own boss.

   c. She just got a new job.

3. a. She wants to take time off from college.

   b. She's planning to do an internship.

   c. She wants to change her major.

B 🔊 **Listen for details.** Read the sentences below. Then listen again. Write one word in each blank and circle the correct answers. **Track 5**

Conversation 1

1. The woman wants to get a degree in _____.

2. She's planning to go this May / in the spring.

Conversation 2

3. The woman is going to do a(n) _____.

4. She's going to make money at some point / right away.

Conversation 3

5. The woman wants to _____ in New York.

6. She plans to do this after graduation / in the near future.

7. She will / won't return to regular classes in September.

C 🔄 Tell a partner: What are the women in each conversation doing or planning to do? Do you know anyone who did any of these things?

> The third woman wants to... My older brother is doing that now.

Many people move to big cities such as New York after graduation.

Word Bank

A *paying position* is a job in which you make money.

A school year is divided into *terms* (for example, the spring and fall term).

3 READING 🔊 Track 6

A 🔄 You have an idea for a new company. You think it will be successful. What should you do? Circle an answer. Then tell a partner.

   a. Get your college degree. After graduation, start your company.

   b. Skip (don't go to) college. Start your company right away.

B **Draw conclusions.** Read paragraphs 1–3 in the reading. How would Peter Thiel answer the question in **A**?

C **Infer meaning.** Find the words in **bold** in the reading. Write each word next to the correct definition.

   1. a teacher or advisor _____

   2. a chance to do something important or interesting _____

   3. did something uncertain or dangerous

     _____

   4. a hidden surprise or problem _____

D **Scan for details.** Find the statements below in paragraphs 1–3. Circle T for *True* and F for *False*. Correct the false statements.

Thiel fellows…

   1. can be any age.   T   F

   2. have to take classes for two years.   T   F

   3. work for free.   T   F

   4. work with special advisors.   T   F

   5. come from all over the world.   T   F

E 🔄 **Identify pros and cons.** What are the pros (good things) and cons (bad things) of being a Thiel fellow? Read paragraphs 4 and 5. Write your ideas on a piece of paper. Compare your answers with a partner's.

F 🔄 Answer the questions with a partner.

   1. What was Eden Full's project? Was she successful?

   2. In your opinion, is the Thiel Fellowship a good idea or not? Why?

A DIFFERENT ROAD TO SUCCESS

1. When Eden Full was 20 years old, she did something unusual: She dropped out[1] of Princeton University. She had an idea for a new kind of technology, an inexpensive kind of solar panel.

2. Full **took a risk** and quit college to work on her idea, but she had help—not from her parents or friends but from billionaire entrepreneur[2] Peter Thiel. In 2010, he created a program called the Thiel Fellowship.[3] It helps people between the ages of 18 and 20 to work on a "big idea." Maybe they want to create a new kind of technology or medicine, or perhaps they want to solve an important social problem. The program gives these young people $100,000 to work on their project for two years. During this time, each person (now called a "fellow") also works with a **mentor**—a successful businessperson, scientist, or inventor. The mentors help the young entrepreneurs.

3. Each year, hundreds of people from around the world apply to the program, but only 20 are accepted. It's an exciting **opportunity**, but there is a **catch**. To be a Thiel fellow, a person must skip or drop out of college. This way, the person can work on his or her project only. He or she won't have to spend time in class or doing homework.

4. For Eden Full, this worked well. She started her project and then returned to Princeton two years later and got her degree. But some people worry about the Thiel Fellowship. Not everyone will be successful, they say. Some projects will fail, and some people won't go back to college.

5. Supporters of the Thiel Fellowship see it differently. The young entrepreneurs will learn a lot. They will also meet important leaders in business, science, and technology, and some will eventually get great jobs. Best of all, some projects will help others—like Eden Full's solar panels, which are now used in nine countries. The reality is this, say supporters: To be successful in life, you have to take risks at some point. Why wait until you're 35? Do it when you're 20.

[1] If you *drop out* of school, you stop going to school.
[2] An *entrepreneur* is a businessperson. Usually he or she starts a new company.
[3] A *fellowship* is a group of people. They share similar interests and work together.

4 GRAMMAR

A Turn to page 69. Complete the exercises. Then do **B** and **C** below.

Predictions with *be going to* and *will*
She**'s going to** / She **will** be very successful.
Some students **aren't going to** / **won't** pass the exam.
He <u>definitely</u> **won't** study history in college.
He**'ll** <u>probably</u> study business.
<u>Maybe</u> he**'ll** study economics, too.
A: **Is** she **going to** / **Will** she go to graduate school?
B: <u>Maybe</u>. / <u>Probably not</u>.

B Read about the two college students. Then think of questions to ask about their futures. Write the questions below.

Education: *Will Naomi get accepted to Stanford?*

Is Alex going to…

Job: _____

_____

Finances (money): _____

_____

Love life: _____

_____

Travel experience: _____

_____

C Take turns asking and answering your questions with a partner. Explain your reasons. At least one answer should use a negative form.

> Will Naomi go back to Sydney someday?

> Yeah, probably. She liked it there.

Naomi is a straight-A student at a very good university. She wants to be a doctor someday. Last summer, she did an internship at a hospital in Sydney, Australia. She loved it there. In Sydney, she dated a guy named Alex, but after she returned home, they broke up. Recently, she applied to Stanford Medical School in the US. She hopes she will be accepted.

Alex is a college student from Sydney, Australia. He's also a talented musician. He's thinking about taking some time off from school. He wants to tour with his band around the world. He also misses his ex-girlfriend, Naomi. They broke up after she returned to her country.

5 WRITING

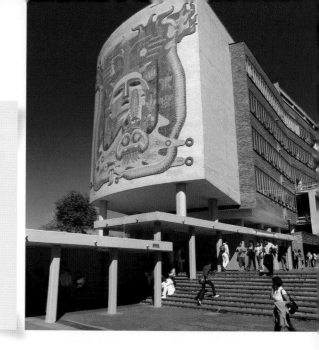

My name is Miguel Sanz. I am a student at the Universidad Nacional Autónoma de Mexico (UNAM) in Mexico City. This May, I am going to graduate with a degree in journalism. **In my third year at UNAM**, I did an internship at *El Universal*, one of Mexico's largest newspapers. There, I worked with senior reporters on different news stories. I also made changes to sports blogs on the paper's website. **In addition to my studies**, I enjoy playing sports, and at UNAM I am on the chess and swim teams. I also like learning languages, and I speak English and some Portuguese.

A 🔄 Read the personal profile above. Then complete the outline about Miguel with a partner.

School: _____

Major: _____

Graduation date: _____

Work experience (when / where / what): _____

School activities: _____

Other abilities: _____

> **i** A personal profile is a short summary (about 100–150 words) of your school and work experience and your abilities.

B Complete the outline in **A** about yourself. The information you write can be real or invented. Then use your ideas and the example to write your own personal profile.

C 🔄 Exchange papers with a partner.

1. Circle any mistakes. Then complete the outline in **A** about your partner on a separate piece of paper.

2. Return the paper to your partner. Make corrections to your own profile.

6 COMMUNICATION

A 🔄 Your instructor is going to give you and a partner two classmates' profiles. Read them and make predictions about each person's future. Write your ideas on the paper.

Our predictions for you

Job:

Finances (money):

Family / Love life:

Travel experiences:

> We think you'll probably... or maybe you'll...

B 🔄 Your instructor will now give you back your paper. Read the predictions you got. Tell a partner: Do you agree with them? Why or why not?

> The first prediction is: You'll probably study in the US at some point.

> Do you think that's true?

> Yeah, probably.

2 STORYTELLING

A group of friends tell stories around a campfire in Yosemite National Park, California, the United States.

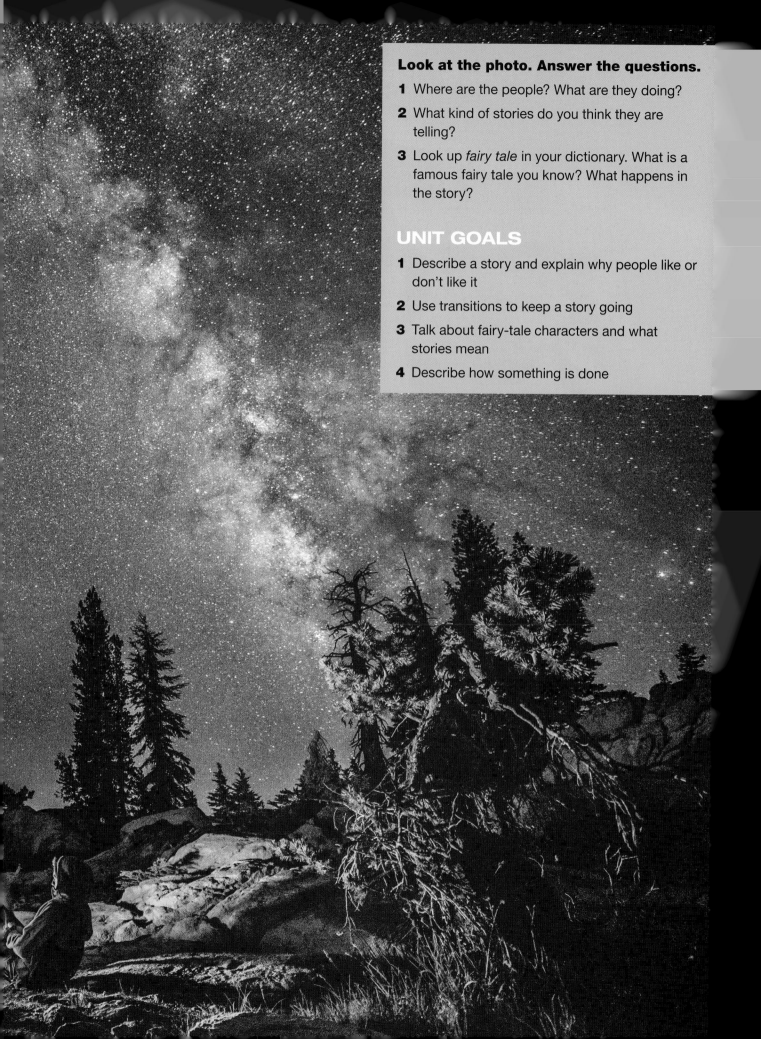

Look at the photo. Answer the questions.

1 Where are the people? What are they doing?

2 What kind of stories do you think they are telling?

3 Look up *fairy tale* in your dictionary. What is a famous fairy tale you know? What happens in the story?

UNIT GOALS

1 Describe a story and explain why people like or don't like it

2 Use transitions to keep a story going

3 Talk about fairy-tale characters and what stories mean

4 Describe how something is done

People dress up as the characters Princess Leia and the stormtroopers from the original *Star Wars* movie.

1 VIDEO Star Wars Subway Car

A Look at the photo. Who are these characters? What do you know about them and about the movie *Star Wars*? Discuss with a partner.

B ▶ Watch the video. Then answer the questions with a partner.

1. Where are the people?

2. What are they doing?

C ▶ Watch the video again. Put the events in order.

_____ Stormtroopers get on the subway.

_____ Darth Vader gets on the subway.

_____ Princess Leia gets on the subway.

_____ Darth Vader and Princess Leia argue.

_____ Princess Leia reads a book.

_____ Everyone gets off the subway.

_____ A stormtrooper grabs Princess Leia.

D Answer the questions with a partner.

1. Who are the people under the costumes? Why are they acting out the *Star Wars* story?

2. The people on the subway are enjoying the *Star Wars* characters. How would you feel if you saw these characters in public?

2 VOCABULARY

A 🔁 With a partner, read about two popular TV shows. Which show is more interesting? Why?

	Game of Thrones (fantasy drama)	*True Detective* (crime drama)
The story	**It tells the story of** three royal families fighting for control of a **made-up** world.	**The story is about** a small team of detectives solving one major crime.
The setting	It takes place hundreds of years ago in a made-up land.	It takes place in the modern-day United States.
The cast	It has one of the largest casts of **characters** on television.	It has a small cast of main characters, and they change every season.
Where the idea came from	It's **based on** a popular **fantasy** book series.	It's created and written by one man.
Why fans say they like it	The characters are exciting to watch, and the story is **unpredictable**.	The quality of the acting is very high, and the story is **realistic**.
Why others say they don't like it	There are too many characters, and the story is **hard to follow**.	The story is too **violent**.

B 🔁 Now think of your favorite TV show. Answer the questions about it on a separate piece of paper. Then tell a partner.

1. What's the name of the show? _____

2. Who are the main characters? _____

3. Where does it take place? _____

4. Is it based on anything? _____

5. What's the story about? _____

_____

6. How would you describe the story?

predictable / unpredictable   easy / hard to follow

realistic / unrealistic   your idea: _____

Word Bank

Word partnerships with *story*

The story is about… / It tells the story of…

a character <u>in</u> a story

tell a story

make up a story

Game of Thrones takes place in a made-up land populated by dragons and other imaginary creatures.

3 LISTENING

Word Bank

contribute = give
something to help
someone

A 🔀 **Infer information.** Answer the questions. Take notes and share your
ideas with a partner.

1. Have you ever heard the word *crowdsourcing* in English?

2. Can you guess the meaning by looking at the two parts of the word: *crowd* and *source*?

B 🔊 **Listen for details.** Listen to the conversation about how crowdsourcing is used to write a story.
Circle the correct answer to complete each sentence. **Track 7**

1. Jamal is working _____.
   a. alone
   b. with a couple of friends
   c. with a lot of people

2. Jamal met the other writers _____.
   a. at school
   b. in writing class
   c. online

3. Each person suggests _____ for the story.
   a. a character
   b. a sentence
   c. an ending

4. The story is _____.
   a. unpredictable
   b. unrealistic
   c. hard to follow

5. Jamal is working on a _____ story.
   a. fantasy
   b. love
   c. crime

6. The story isn't _____.
   a. realistic
   b. true
   c. well known

C 🔀 Look at your notes in **A** and your answers in **B**. What is a crowdsourced story?
Complete the summary below. Compare your answers with a partner's.

Part of Jamal's story takes place in Madrid. What
place do you think would make a good story setting?

To create a crowdsourced story, (1.) _____ work
together. They don't work in an office. They work
(2.) _____. Everyone contributes (3.) _____.

The people don't (4.) _____ each other, and they
don't receive any (5.) _____ for their work.

D 🔀 Discuss the questions with a partner.

1. Do you think crowdsourcing is good or bad?

2. Do you think crowdsourcing is a good way to
   tell a story?

4 SPEAKING

A 🔊 **Pronunciation: Compound words.** Here are more words used to describe stories. Look up the ones you don't know in your dictionary. Then listen and repeat. Pay attention to the stress. **Track 8**

1. heartbreaking   2. heartwarming   3. uplifting

B 🔊 Mia is telling Nico a story. Listen and then answer the questions about the story. **Track 9**

1. How many characters are in the story?

2. Where does it take place?

3. What happened? Was the story easy to follow?

4. This is an example of a *feel-good* story. What do you think that means?

MIA: Wow, I just heard an amazing story.

NICO: Yeah? What's it about?

MIA: It's a story about a waitress. She had a lot of money problems.

NICO: That sounds hard.

MIA: It is. Anyway, she found out she was losing her apartment. She had to move, but she didn't have enough money.

NICO: Oh no!

MIA: As it turns out, she told one of her customers about the situation. This customer was special. He came to the restaurant often and knew the waitress well. And he wanted to help her.

NICO: So what did he do?

MIA: One day he paid his bill and left the restaurant, as usual. When the waitress went to collect her tip, she found a $3,000 tip... on a bill of $43.50!

NICO: Are you serious?

MIA: I am. It's a true story. And in the end, the waitress was OK.

NICO: What a heartwarming story. I'm glad it had a happy ending.

> ℹ️ When eating out in North America, it is customary to tip your server an extra 20 percent for service after you have finished eating your meal.

C 🔁 Practice the conversation with a partner.

SPEAKING STRATEGY

D 🔁 On a piece of paper, write a word or single sentence for each item below. Then exchange papers with a partner. Use your partner's notes and the Useful Expressions to write a story.

1. a person's name

2. another person's name

3. a place

4. how the two people met

5. what happened to the two people

Useful Expressions
Keeping a story going
One day,…
So, (then),…
Later,…
After that,…
As it turns out,…
It turns out that,…

E 🔁 Work with a new partner and do the following:

Student A: Tell your story.

Student B: Listen. Tell your partner what you liked about the story.

> My story is about a student named Jonah. Something amazing happened to him.

> What happened?

F 🔁 Switch roles and do **E** again.

5 GRAMMAR

A Turn to pages 70–71. Complete the exercises. Then do **B** and **C** below.

The Past Continuous Tense: Statements				
Subject	***was / were (not)***	**Verb + *ing***		
I / He / She	was(n't)	**studying**	English	at four o'clock.
You / We / They	were(n't)			last summer.
				after lunchtime.

The Past Continuous Tense: Questions						
	***Wh-* word**	***was / were***	**Subject**	**Verb + *ing***		**Answers**
Yes / No Questions		Were	you	**reading**	a story?	Yes, I was. / No, I wasn't.
***Wh-* Questions**	What	were	you	**reading**?		(I was **reading**) a story.

B Unscramble the questions and their answers.

1. were / doing / at / what / you / last night / 8:00 _____

   Game of Thrones / watching / I / on TV / was _____

2. yesterday / friend / was / what / wearing / best / your _____

   _____

   wearing / school / her / she / uniform / was _____

3. your / were / phone / talking / earlier / you / cell / on _____

   _____

   wasn't / no, / I _____

   lunch / was / I / eating _____

4. studying / was / your / yesterday / class / what _____

   were / *World Link* / grammar / we / studying / in _____

5. summer / family / was / your / traveling / last _____

   were / we / yes, _____

   to / went / Spain / we _____

C 🔁 Ask and answer the questions in **B** with a partner. Give answers that are true for you. Then think of a follow-up question to ask a partner.

> What were you doing last night at 8:00?

> I was studying at home in my room.

> How long were you studying?

> For about three hours. I was preparing for a big test.

6 COMMUNICATION

A 🔊 You are going to hear two people talk about a car accident. One person is lying. Listen to each person's story and take notes below. **Track 10**

	Jenna	Ryan
When did it happen?		
Where did it happen?		
What happened?		
What color was the car?		
Who was driving?		

B 🔄 Circle your answers below. Discuss your ideas with a partner.

1. Jenna / Ryan remembers the details clearly.

2. Jenna / Ryan sounds more confident.

3. Jenna / Ryan hesitates more.

4. I think Jenna / Ryan is making up the story.

C 🔄 Think about something funny or unusual that happened to you. Then follow the steps below with a partner.

1. **Student A:** Tell your story.
   Student B: Listen and take notes on *who*, *what*, *where*, *when*, and *why*.

2. Switch roles and repeat step 1.

3. Now choose <u>one</u> of your stories.

4. Think of ways that you can make the story untrue, for example, changing the details. Write down another version of the story with the untrue parts.

D 👥 Get together with another pair.

- **Pair 1:** One of you will tell the story as it really happened to you. The other person will tell the story with the made-up parts. Begin with each person saying one sentence of their story. Take turns telling the rest of the story, one sentence at a time.

- **Pair 2:** Ask each person in Pair 1 questions about their story. You have one minute. Then guess: Who is telling the truth and who is making up the story? How do you know?

> I was walking to work one day when I met someone famous.

> *I* was walking to the store one day when I met someone famous.

> OK, let me start with Person 1. You said you were walking to work. Where exactly do you work?

E 👥 Switch roles and do **D** again.

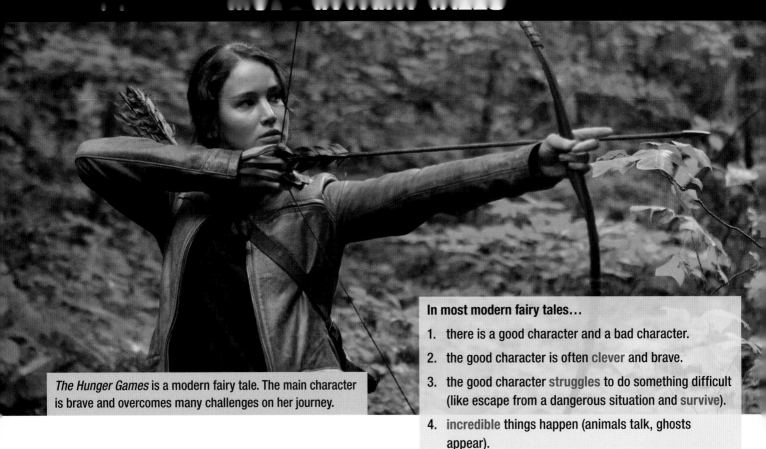

The Hunger Games is a modern fairy tale. The main character is brave and overcomes many challenges on her journey.

In most modern fairy tales…

1. there is a good character and a bad character.

2. the good character is often **clever** and brave.

3. the good character **struggles** to do something difficult (like escape from a dangerous situation and **survive**).

4. **incredible** things happen (animals talk, ghosts appear).

5. the good character **overcomes** the difficult situation and succeeds.

6. the good character often **discovers** something important about life.

7. the story usually ends happily.

1 VOCABULARY

A The movie in the photo is an example of a modern fairy tale. Can you guess why? Tell a partner. Then take turns reading sentences 1–7 aloud.

B Match the correct form of each word in **blue** in sentences 1–7 with a definition below.

1. to deal with a difficult situation successfully ___*overcome*___

2. intelligent _____

3. to learn something you didn't know in the past _____

4. hard to believe _____

5. to try hard to do something difficult _____

6. to stay alive in a difficult situation _____

C Work with a partner. Follow the steps below.

1. Choose a modern fairy tale to talk about.

2. Are sentences 1–7 true about the story? Explain.

3. Do you like the story? Why or why not?

4. Switch roles and repeat 1–3.

Examples of modern fairy tales

The Hunger Games   *Star Wars*

Harry Potter   Your idea: _____

> In *The Hunger Games*, Katniss Everdeen is the good character. She's clever and brave. For example…

2 LISTENING

A 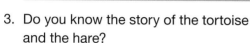 **Build background knowledge; Make predictions.** Answer the questions with a partner.

1. What do the words in the box below mean?

2. Which words do you think describe the animals in the picture?

a hare

a tortoise

arrogant	patient	quick	slow

3. Do you know the story of the tortoise and the hare?

B 🔊 **Listen for main ideas.** Marnie and her dad are talking. Read the sentences. Then listen and circle the correct answer(s). **Track 11**

1. There's a contest / game / test at school, and Marnie thinks she's going to fail / lose / win.

2. Laura Sanders is Marnie's friend / competitor / teacher.

3. Laura is very talented / funny / kind.

C 🔊 **Listen for details.** Marnie's dad tells her the story *The Tortoise and the Hare*. Listen and write *H* for hare and *T* for tortoise. **Track 12**

1. The _____ challenges the _____.

2. The _____ thinks he will win the race.

3. The _____ takes a rest during the race.

4. The _____ finishes the race first.

5. The _____ was arrogant.

6. The _____ was clever.

D 🔊 **Summarize.** Listen again. Marnie's dad is giving her some advice by telling the story. What is his advice? Listen again. Then list your ideas. **Track 12**

Marnie's dad gives her this advice: _____

_____

E 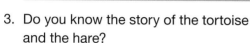 Answer the questions with a partner.

1. Why does Marnie's dad tell her the story?

2. Do you agree with her dad's advice?

3. Can you think of another old or traditional story that can still "teach a lesson" about life?

A 🔄 **Use background knowledge.** Look at the title and the photo. What do you know about the fairy-tale character Cinderella? Tell a partner.

B **Identify main ideas.** Read the passage. Then write the headers below in the correct places in the reading. Two are extra.

One story, many cultures

Cinderella in the movies

Why we love her

A present-day Cinderella

The African Cinderella

A famous fairy tale

C **Scan for details.** Match the names (1–5) with the answers (a–f) to make true sentences. One answer is extra.

1. The African Cinderella _____
2. Becan _____
3. Cindy Ella _____
4. The Filipina Cinderella _____
5. Settareh _____

a. attends a New Year's party.
b. has a forest spirit help her.
c. has only one stepsister.
d. is a boy "Cinderella."
e. was a movie version of the Cinderella story.
f. is an unpopular high school student.

D 🔄 Answer the questions with a partner.

1. Why is the Cinderella story so popular? The reading lists three reasons. Do you agree with them?

2. Is there a Cinderella story in your country? If so, what is the story?

THE CINDERELLA STORY

1. _____

The Cinderella story is a famous one. Cinderella was living happily with her family when her mother died. Her father remarried. Cinderella's new stepmother and two stepsisters treated her poorly. She had to wear old clothes and work hard while the sisters wore beautiful clothes and had fun.

You know the rest of the story. A good fairy[1] helped Cinderella. She turned Cinderella's old clothes into a beautiful dress. Cinderella went to a party, and a prince fell in love with her. Cinderella left the party quickly and didn't tell the prince her name. But she did leave a glass slipper, and the prince used that to find her. Eventually, Cinderella and the prince married and lived happily ever after.

2. _____

That's one telling of the story, but the Cinderella fairy tale is found in many different countries with some differences. In an African version, for example, there is one stepsister, not two. In a version from the Philippines, a forest spirit helps the Cinderella character. Settareh, a Middle Eastern Cinderella, goes to a New Year's party. And Cinderella is not always a woman. In an Irish story, a young boy, Becan, marries a princess and lives happily ever after.

3. _____

There are also modern retellings of the Cinderella story. In one, a girl named Cindy Ella is a student at a Los Angeles high school. Her fashionable stepmother and older stepsisters care a lot about shopping and money. Cindy doesn't. When she writes a letter to her school newspaper against a school dance, she becomes very unpopular with both students and teachers. Only her two best friends— and later the school's most handsome boy—support her.

4. _____

Why is the Cinderella story so popular and found in so many cultures? There are a few reasons. First of all, it's a romantic story, which is a popular style. Also, Cinderella is a kind girl with a hard life. People want her to succeed. But maybe the most important reason is that in the Cinderella story, a person struggles, but overcomes the difficulties in the end. That's a story that everyone—boy or girl, young or old—wants to believe can happen.

[1] A *fairy* is a person with magical power.

Cinderella and the prince dance at the party.

4 GRAMMAR

A Turn to page 72. Complete the exercises. Then do **B–E** below.

Adverbs of Manner	
Cinderella smiled **shyly** at the prince.	**Adverbs of manner** describe how something is done. Many end in *-ly,* and they often come after a verb.
He opened <u>the door</u> **quietly**. She answered <u>the question</u> **correctly**.	When there is <u>an object</u> (a noun or pronoun) after the verb, the adverb usually comes at the end of the sentence.
She was <u>different</u> from other children. You seem <u>unhappy</u>.	<u>Adjectives</u>, not adverbs, come after stative verbs (words like *be, have, hear, know, seem*).
She drives too **fast**. He studied **hard** for the exam. They didn't do **well** in school.	Some adverbs of manner don't end in *-ly*.

B 🗘 Circle the adjective or adverb to complete the profile. Then take turns reading the story aloud with a partner.

As a child in the UK, Daniel Tammet was different / differently from other children. As a boy, he liked to play alone and acted strange / strangely around others. In school, he struggled to do good / well. To many of his classmates, Daniel seemed unusual / unusually, and they laughed at him. This hurt Daniel deep / deeply, and he became very shy / shyly.

As a teenager, Daniel discovered he had an incredible ability. He could solve difficult math problems almost instant / instantly. He also discovered another talent: he could learn to speak a language very quick / quickly. Today, he is fluent / fluently in ten languages.

As an adult, Daniel overcame his shyness. He wrote three books in which he speaks eloquent / eloquently about his life and ideas.

Word Bank
An *eloquent* speaker talks in a clear and powerful way.

C 🗘 Take turns asking and answering the questions with a partner.

1. As a child, how did Daniel act? Why?
2. How did people treat Daniel? How did this make him feel?
3. What two special abilities does Daniel have?
4. Does Daniel's story end happily? Why or why not?

D 👥 Get into a small group. Add four verbs and two adverbs to the chart.

Verbs		Adverbs	
climb	talk	calmly	patiently
dance	_____	carefully	quiet
laugh	_____	gracefully	terribly
run	_____	happily	_____
sing	_____	nervously	_____

E 👥 Choose a verb and an adverb. Then act out the combination. Can your group guess what you're doing? Take turns with the people in your group.

> You're singing terribly!

5 WRITING

A Look at the picture from the Cinderella story. Answer the questions with a partner.

1. Who are the characters?
2. Where are they?
3. How do you think each person feels?

B Imagine it is the day after the party. Choose a character from the picture. Write an email in that character's words to a friend about the party. You can make up information, including other characters. See the example to the right. In your message, write at least eight sentences. Use three adverbs of manner. Also pay attention to your use of the simple past and past continuous tenses.

C Exchange papers with a partner. Did he or she follow the directions in **B**? Circle any mistakes. Then give the paper back to your partner.

> Last night, my parents had a big party at a hotel downtown for my father's friends and coworkers. I didn't want to go, but I had to. At first, the party was incredibly boring. I waited patiently for an hour, and then I decided to leave. But then, when I was walking out, an amazing girl arrived and the whole night changed...

6 COMMUNICATION

A Work in a small group. One person begins. Read your message from Writing **B** to the group. Act it out with feeling. When you listen, guess: Who is the speaker?

B Were the stories with the same characters from **A** the same or different? Which one did you like the most?

3 TECHNOLOGY

Artist Nick Gentry uses old technology (such as these floppy disks) to create portraits.

Look at the photo. Answer the questions.

1 What old technology is in the picture?

2 Do you know what they were used for? Guess.

3 How has technology improved our lives in the last ten years? Name one way.

UNIT GOALS

1 Describe a gadget

2 Describe how things used to be

3 Talk about events in the past that no longer happen

4 Compare similar items

The Apple II personal computer came out in 1977. It was one of the first bestsellers in the computer industry.

1 VIDEO Kids React to Old Computers

A Look at the computer in the photo. How have computers changed since then? Think of one or two ways. Tell a partner.

B Look up any words you don't know. Then watch the video. Check (✓) the items you see.

☐ an error message   ☐ a monitor   ☐ a keyboard   ☐ a mouse

☐ an on switch   ☐ a screen   ☐ a printer

C Read the kids' statements below and try to guess the answers. Then watch the video again and check your answers.

button	desk	Internet	nothing	programs	televisions

1. Jayka: "If you don't have a _____, where do you put this?"

2. Tyler: "It's kind of like those old _____ that are very boxy."

3. Brooke-Monaé: "Apps! Games! Websites! Everything! But this thing right here has _____!"

4. Narrator: "You can't do anything, or even type until you hit a reset _____."

5. Dylan: "Are there any _____ on it?"

6. Narrator: "How do you go on the _____?"

D How did the kids feel about the old computer? How do you feel about it? Discuss with a partner.

2 VOCABULARY

Trying to get in shape? The BeFit makes your goals more **manageable** by tracking your exercise, activity patterns, and diet. This **remarkable** product tells time *and* helps you use your time well!

Product features

- It's **portable** and goes with you everywhere, so it gives you a **reliable** and complete picture of your daily activity.

- The BeFit is **dependable**: It performs perfectly even during your most intense workout!

- The BeFit comes in a variety of colors, so it is always **fashionable**.

Product reviews

Fitgurl2018 I started using a BeFit as a **practical** way to help me lose weight... I love it!

NotSoSure A lot of people are excited about this product, but it's not very **affordable**. It's too much money!

SaveYour$$! This is not as **durable** as they say... I wore mine to the beach, and now it doesn't work!

> **i** Remember, the suffixes *–able / -ible / -ble* mean *capable of* or *can*. If something is *affordable*, you can afford it (it is not too expensive).

A Read the ad above. Pay attention to the words in **blue**. Check (✓) True or False.

If something is…	True	False		True	False
1. *affordable*, it's expensive.	☐	☐	5. *durable*, it breaks easily.	☐	☐
2. *remarkable*, it's not special.	☐	☐	6. *portable*, you can carry it easily.	☐	☐
3. *practical*, it's useful and logical.	☐	☐	7. *reliable*, you can trust it.	☐	☐
4. *manageable*, it's difficult to control.	☐	☐	8. *fashionable*, it is in style.	☐	☐

B 🔁 Check your answers in **A** with a partner. For the false statements, write correct definitions.

C 🔁 Answer the questions with a partner.

1. What do you like about the BeFit?

2. Would you ever use a product like this? Why or why not?

3. Think of a gadget you own. Which words in blue from **A** would you use to describe it?

> I think my phone is really practical. I can do a lot of things on it.

The Model T was one of the first cars available to many people, helping to make automobiles popular.

A 🔁 Look at the words in the Word Bank. What do they mean? What is one recent fad? Tell a partner.

Word Bank
a fad = something popular for a short time
a flash in the pan = something successful for a short time

B 🔊 **Listen for the main idea.** You are going to hear a lecture. Listen and choose the best title for the lecture. **Track 14**

Guessing the Future: Predictions about technology that were _____.

a. remarkable
c. wrong

b. creative
d. confusing

C 🔊 **Listen for details; Note taking.** Listen to the full lecture. Complete the missing information in the chart. **Track 15**

Word Bank
one billion = 1,000,000,000

Year	Device	Prediction (then)	Description (now)	Number
1876	telephone	_____ _____ the telephone, but we do not.	indispensable	
____	automobile	The _____ is here to stay, but the automobile is a _____.	_____ _____	more than _____ billion cars
____	television	Television won't _____. It's just a _____ in the _____.	_____	around _____ billion TVs
____	Internet	The Internet will _____.		over _____ billion users

D 🔁 Choose one of the devices from **C** and predict how it will be different 20 years from now and 50 years from now. Tell a partner. Do you agree with his or her predictions? Why or why not?

4 SPEAKING

A 🔊 💬 Listen to Alan and Kim's conversation. Then answer the questions with a partner. **Track 16**

1. How would most people describe Kim's sister?

2. What is Kim's sister really like?

ALAN: Hey, Kim. I saw your sister on Facebook the other day. She's really changed a lot.

KIM: Yeah? Why do you say that? She still looks the same.

ALAN: Yeah, but now she's got all these friends, and she's really funny. She used to be so different— you know, kind of shy.

KIM: A lot of people say that about my sister. They think that she's this quiet person, but, actually, she's very outgoing.

ALAN: Really?

KIM: Yep. Once she feels comfortable with you, she's really friendly, and she talks a lot.

ALAN: Wow, I had no idea.

B 💬 Practice the conversation with a partner. Do you know anyone like Kim's sister?

SPEAKING STRATEGY

Useful Expressions: Offering a Counterargument		
Stating what other people think	A lot of people say (that)...	she's really shy.
	Some people think (that)...	
Explaining what you think	(But,) actually,...	she's very outgoing.
	(But,) in fact, / in reality,...	
	(But,) the truth / fact / reality is...	

C Read the statements below and check (✓) the ones you agree with.

☐ Learning English is easy.

☐ Modern technology is always reliable.

☐ Everybody should get married someday.

☐ Wearing black is always fashionable.

☐ Activity trackers, such as the BeFit, are affordable.

☐ The apps on your phone should be practical.

D 💬 With a partner, compare your opinions about the statements in **C**. Talk about the statements you <u>don't</u> agree with. Use the Useful Expressions to help you.

> Some people say learning English is easy, but, actually, it's hard.

> Why do you say that?

E 💬 Tell a partner something surprising about you or your country.

> A lot of people think it's warm in Spain all year, but, in reality, it's very cold in the winter.

> Well, for one thing, there's the grammar. It's complex and...

5 GRAMMAR

A Turn to pages 73–74. Complete the exercises. Then do **B–E** below.

Used to			
Subject	***use(d) to***	**Verb**	
I	**used to**	wear	glasses.
She	didn't **use to**	own	a computer.

Did	**Subject**	***use to***	**Verb**		**Responses**
Did	you	**use to**	wear	glasses?	Yes, I did. / No, I didn't.
	she		own	a computer?	Yes, she did. / No, she didn't.

B 🔊 Pronunciation: *Used to.* Listen to the sentences. Notice the different pronunciation of the *s* in *used* / *use to* and the *s* in the verb forms *use* / *used*. **Track 17**

used / use to: s = /s/   use / used: s = /z/

1. People <u>used</u> to go to movie theaters a lot more.

2. I didn't <u>use</u> to shop online.

3. What kind of computer do you <u>use</u>?

4. I <u>used</u> my brother's cell phone.

C 🔊 🔁 Pronunciation: *Used to.* Listen to how the words *use* and *used* are pronounced. Check (✓) /s/ or /z/. Then take turns reading the sentences aloud with a partner. **Track 18**

                                /s/   /z/   /s/   /z/

1. She used the phone in her office. ☐ ☐   3. Do you use a tablet? ☐ ☐

2. My email used to be more manageable. ☐ ☐   4. I didn't use to eat meat. ☐ ☐

D 🔁 Unscramble the sentences. Then ask and answer the questions with a partner.

1. use to / you / somewhere else / did / live _____?

2. go / you / use to / to a different school / did _____?

3. use / did / use to / pay phones / people _____?

4. did / have / you / long hair / use to _____?

5. wear / did / use to / you / a watch _____?

E 👥 Follow the steps below.

1. Write down three true statements on three pieces of paper about things you used to do.

2. Give the papers to your instructor.

3. Your instructor will give you three pieces of paper with statements from your classmates.

4. Walk around the class and ask questions to find out who the papers belong to.

> Did you use to ride your bike to school everyday?

> Yes, I did, but it took forever! Now I take the bus to school.

6 COMMUNICATION

A 🔄 Three years ago, Tetsuya and his family moved from Tokyo to Los Angeles. Look at his old Tokyo profile (on the left) and his new Los Angeles profile (on the right). How has his life changed? With a partner, make sentences with *used to* and *didn't use to*.

> People used to call him Tetsuya. Now everyone calls him...

Three years ago

Tetsuya
Tokyo

About

My name is Tetsuya.

I live in Tokyo with my parents.

I wear a uniform to school.

I ride my bicycle to school.

I don't belong to any clubs at school.

I don't have many chances to practice my English.

Today

Ted
Los Angeles

About

Everyone here calls me "Ted."

I live in an apartment in L.A. with two roommates.

It's warm here. I wear a T-shirt almost every day!

I have a car! I drive to college.

I'm a member of the swim team.

I speak English all the time.

B Make notes about your life five years ago and now. Try to write down things that are different, if possible.

Five years ago	Now
Home: _____	Home: _____
Family: _____	Family: _____
Friends: _____	Friends: _____
Work / school: _____	Work / school: _____
Favorite activities: _____	Favorite activities: _____
Favorite TV shows / movies: _____	Favorite TV shows / movies: _____
Other: _____	Other: _____

C 🔄 Tell your partner how your life has changed in the past five years. Whose life—yours or your partner's—has changed the most?

> I still live in the same apartment, but my family situation has changed.

> My older brother used to live at home, but now he's away at college.

> How so?

Great Pacific Garbage Patch map

1 VOCABULARY

The Great Pacific Garbage Patch is an area **located** in the Pacific Ocean. It is hundreds of kilometers wide and is filled with trash—most of which is plastic.

Eventually, this area may **have a negative effect** on humans. For example, fish that **consume** plastic because they think it is food won't be safe to eat.

Scientists are trying to **prevent** the growth of this area. They think we can prevent the growth of this area if we use less plastic and **recycle** any plastic we already have. They are also trying to **rescue** injured or sick animals in the area and use advanced technology to **transform** the plastic so that it breaks down faster. In time, this will **reduce** the amount of plastic in the area to almost nothing. Eventually, scientists hope to **restore** the area to its original state.

A Read the information. Then match a word or phrase in **blue** with its definition below.

1. stop something from happening _____

2. decrease _____

3. save _____

4. reuse _____

5. eat or drink _____

6. change something completely _____

7. have a bad influence _____

8. found in a certain place _____

9. make something like it was in the past _____

B Read the information in **A** again. Then with a partner, take turns answering these questions.

1. What and where is the Great Pacific Garbage Patch?

2. Why is this area a problem?

3. What are scientists doing about the problem?

4. In addition to recycling, how else can we reduce the amount of plastic we use?

2 LISTENING

 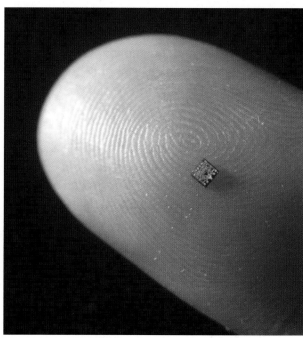

A Complete the sentences with the words *blind*, *sight*, and *vision*. Use your dictionary to help you.

1. _____ or _____ is the ability to see things.

2. If you are _____, you can't see.

B 🔊 **Listen for gist and details.** Look at the photos and read the sentences below. Then listen and choose the best answer to complete each one. **Track 19**

1. The man is talking about a tool he and others are working on. This tool will _____.

   a. prevent blindness from happening

   b. restore blind people's vision

   c. give blind people perfect vision

2. The glasses have a _____ inside.

   a. computer chip   b. pen   c. video camera

C 🔊 **Listen to sequence events.** How does the tool work? Read the sentences below. Then listen again and put the steps in the order (1–5) they happen. **Track 19**

_____ The person can see the pen.

_____ The blind person puts on special glasses and looks at an object, such as a pen.

_____ The picture is sent to the chip in the person's eye.

_____ Doctors put a computer chip in a blind person's eye.

_____ The glasses take a picture of the pen.

D 🔁 Use your answers in **B** and **C** to explain how this new technology works. What do you think of this tool? Tell a partner.

READING 🔊 Track 20

A 🔁 **Make predictions.** Read the title of the news article. Then look at the photo and read the caption. What do you think this article is about? Tell a partner. Then read the article to check your ideas.

B **Infer meaning.** Find the four underlined words in the passage and read the sentences they are in. Then match each word with its definition. One definition is extra.

1. collapsed _____
2. trapped _____
3. position _____
4. identified _____

a. discovered
b. put something down
c. fell down
d. unable to escape or move
e. location, place

C **Sequence events.** Morgan is telling people what happened. Number the events (1–9) in the order they happened.

_____ They took me to the hospital.

_____ Then the roof of the gym fell down, and I passed out.

_____ I went to the gym for my class.

_____ I have to stay for a couple of days, but I'm feeling much better!

_____ Then suddenly, this little robot appeared.

__1__ It was snowing really hard on Tuesday morning.

_____ A couple of men found me.

_____ When I woke up, I tried to move, but I couldn't. I was scared.

_____ I heard this really loud sound.

D 🔁 In what other kinds of situations could rescue robots be used? Tell a partner.

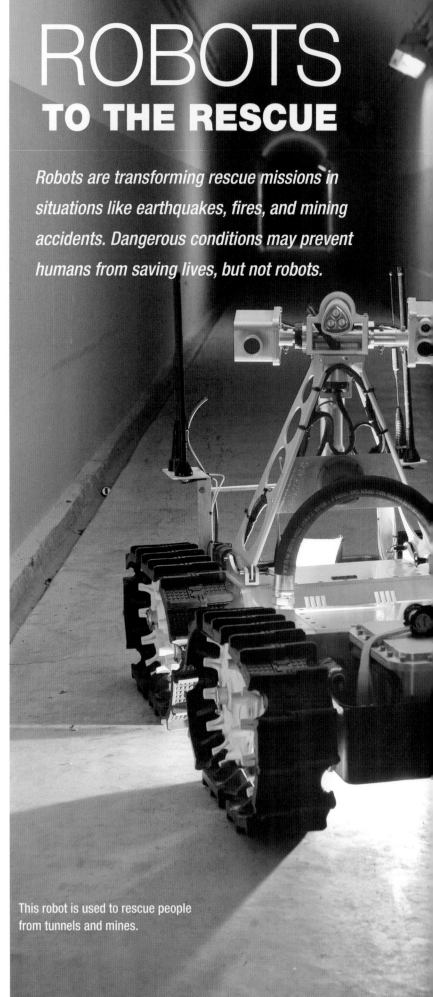

ROBOTS
TO THE RESCUE

Robots are transforming rescue missions in situations like earthquakes, fires, and mining accidents. Dangerous conditions may prevent humans from saving lives, but not robots.

This robot is used to rescue people from tunnels and mines.

1 She may have a broken leg, but she couldn't be happier. Morgan Bailey, 15, is lucky to be alive.

It seemed like a normal Tuesday for Morgan. She was at school. It was fourth period, and she was the first student to arrive in the
5 gymnasium for her physical education class.

Suddenly there was a loud noise.

"There was a sharp, cracking noise and then a loud boom. After that, I don't remember anything," said Morgan. "I guess I passed out.[1]"

10 The roof of the gymnasium had <u>collapsed</u> under the heavy snow. Morgan was <u>trapped</u> underneath. She couldn't escape.

"I woke up and there was a big piece of wood on my leg. I couldn't move it. I was starting to get cold."

Fortunately, help was nearby. A new program using rescue
15 robots was tried for the first time.

"We were nervous about using the robot," said Derrick Sneed, the man in charge of the program. "But in the end, the robot gave us reliable information. It went extremely well."

The rescue robot was able to go into the gym and locate
20 Morgan's exact <u>position</u>.

"We send in robots first because it's just more practical. A situation may not be safe for humans," said Mr. Sneed. A gas leak,[2] for example, could kill you or me, but wouldn't hurt a robot."

Although it didn't happen in Morgan's case, some rescue robots
25 can bring fresh air or water to people who are trapped.

"Once we <u>identified</u> Morgan's location and knew it was safe to go in, a couple of our men went in to rescue her," says Sneed. "Her leg was broken and she was scared, but thankfully, she was alive."

Doctors sent Morgan home from the hospital after only two
30 days. What's the first thing she wanted to do? "I wanted to meet my hero!" Morgan laughs. "That little robot saved my life!"

[1]If you *pass out*, you become unconscious.
[2]When a *gas leak* happens, the air is not safe to breathe.

4 GRAMMAR

A Turn to pages 74–75. Complete the exercises. Then do **B** and **C** below.

Comparisons with *as... as*

Phone A is 12 centimeters. Phone B is 12 centimeters.
   Phone A is **as** <u>big</u> **as** phone B.
Phone A costs $100. Phone B costs $100.
   Phone A costs **as** <u>much</u> **as** phone B.

Camera A isn't **as** <u>affordable</u> **as** Camera B.
Maria didn't do **as** <u>well</u> **as** Carlos on the test.

B Read about the two cars. Then, with a partner, make sentences using *(not) as... as* about them. Which car do you think is better?

Both the Fiat and Tesla are electric cars.

	Car 1: Fiat 500e	Car 2: Tesla Model S
price	$32,000	$100,000+
durability	lasts 5+ years	lasts 5+ years
popularity	very popular	only with the rich

> They're both electric cars, but the Tesla isn't as affordable as the Fiat.

C With your partner, complete the chart with two more electronic devices (for example, two different phones, two different tablets). In your opinion, which product is better? Explain with sentences using *(not) as... as.*

	1: _____	2: _____
price		
size		
durability		
popularity		

5 WRITING

A 🔁 Read the paragraph. What two things is the writer comparing? Which one does she like more? Why? Tell a partner.

B Look at the two products you compared in Grammar **C**. Choose one and in a paragraph explain which product you think is better.

C 🔁 Exchange papers with a partner.

1. Answer the questions in **A** about your partner's writing.

2. Circle any mistakes in your partner's writing. Then return the paper to your partner. Make changes to your own paper.

> I used to own a BeFit activity tracker, but two months ago, I got an iLife. Of the two activity trackers, I like the iLife better for a couple of reasons. First, the iLife lets me do a lot of things. I can track my activity. I can also see who is calling me, set alarms for myself, and many other things. The BeFit doesn't have as many features. Second, the BeFit uses a lot of power, so its battery doesn't last as long as the iLife's. For these two reasons, I think the iLife is a better product.

6 COMMUNICATION

A 🔁 With a partner, design a robot that will do something useful for people. Discuss the questions below.

Name of our robot: _____

1. What is the purpose of the robot? Choose from the list below or write your own idea.

be a friend to children / adults	do household chores
work in schools	work in hospitals
do factory work / build things	your idea: _____

2. What exactly will the robot do?

3. What will the robot look like? Draw a simple picture on a separate piece of paper.

4. Why is the robot as good as (or better than) a human?

5. How much will the robot cost?

B 👥 Get together with another pair and take turns doing the following.

Presenters: Present your robot. Start by saying its name.

Listeners: As you listen to the other pair's presentation, answer questions 1–5 in **A**. At the end of the presentation, you may ask questions.

> Today, we're going to tell you about our robot, Robbie. He works in...

C 👥 Repeat **B** with two other pairs. At the end, compare notes with your partner and choose your favorite robot. Explain your choice to the class.

Paro is a Japanese robotic toy used in hospitals. It looks like a seal and helps to reduce stress in patients.

4 TELEPHONING

Look at the photo. Answer the questions.

1 What are these people doing?

2 Do you ever have to do this?

3 What kind of phone do you have now? Do you like it?

UNIT GOALS

1 Use formal and informal language on the phone

2 Talk about phone etiquette

3 Discuss plans and opinions

4 Describe your personal phone habits

In the country of Djibouti, migrants from Somalia search for a phone signal in order to call home.

1 VIDEO A Conference Call in Real Life

A 🔁 What are the challenges of holding a conference call with people in many different places? Discuss with a partner.

B ▶ Read about the challenges of conference calls below. Then watch and check off the ones you see in the video.

Word Bank

A *conference call* or *teleconference* is a telephone meeting for people in different locations. Each person *joins the meeting* by calling in on a separate phone, entering an *access code*, and saying their name.

The challenges of conference calls

☐ Some people are late in joining the call.

☐ The conversation can be awkward.

☐ The calls are too expensive.

☐ There are too many outside interruptions.

☐ People talk at the same time.

☐ No one leads the call.

☐ You can't hear well.

☐ Some people leave the call early.

C 🔁 Do you think conference calls are useful? Why or why not? Discuss with a partner.

2 VOCABULARY

Word Bank
Phrases with *phone*
answer the phone ↔ hang up the phone
turn on your phone ↔ turn off your phone
mute / silence your phone
be on the phone / talk on the phone
borrow / use someone's phone
Phrases with *call*
call someone / make a call
call someone back / return a call
get a call from someone
screen your calls
Phrases with *message*
get a (text / phone) message ↔
leave a message[1] / send a message[2]
check your (text / phone) messages
take a message

[1]You *leave* a (voice) message on the phone.   [2]You *send* text messages.

A Look at the Word Bank. Use a dictionary to look up any words you don't know.

B Use the Word Bank to complete the dialogs below. Use the correct form of the verb. In some cases, more than one answer may be possible.

1. A: Emily just called. She's running five minutes late.

   B: Really? But the movie is starting in five minutes!

   A: Let's _____ her a text message. Now, what should we tell her?

2. A: Hello, is Mr. Choi there?

   B: He is, but he's _____ the phone right now.

   A: Oh, OK. Can I _____ a message for him?

3. A: Your phone is ringing. Are you going to _____ it?

   B: No, I'm not. I'm _____ my calls.

   A: I see. Who are you trying to avoid?

4. A: Can I _____ your phone for a second?

   B: Sure. Here you go.

   A: Thanks. I have to _____ a couple of calls right away.

5. A: Your phone is beeping. I think you need to _____ your text messages.

   B: You're right. Wow! I just _____ 13 new messages!

   A: Really? Who are they from?

C Work with a partner. Choose one of the dialogs in **B**. Add two more lines to it. Then perform your dialog for another pair.

3 LISTENING

A 🔊 **Pronunciation: Stress in clarification questions.** Listen to the dialog. Notice the intonation of B's sentence. Why does B stress the underlined number? **Track 21**

A: My number is 555-6749.

B: 555-6749?

A: Yes. 6-7-4-9.

B 🔊 **Pronunciation: Stress in clarification questions.** Listen and complete the dialogs. **Track 22**

1. A: My Skype username is nancy_p12.

   B: Did you say _____?

   A: No, p12. That's p as in *Paul*.

2. A: My username is @photoguy.

   B: _____?

   A: That's correct.

3. A: My email address is joym@sf.edu.

   B: Was that _____ at sf.edu?

   A: No, it's joy m as in *Mary*.

Many people use Skype to communicate with friends, family, and coworkers around the world.

ℹ️ How to say these symbols:
@ = at
_ = underscore
# = hashtag

C 🔁 Practice the dialogs in **B** with a partner. Then use your own information and practice again.

D 🔊 **Make predictions; Infer information.** Read the sentences below. Then listen to six dialogs. In each dialog, what could be said next? Choose the best response. **Track 23**

1. a. OK, I'll check my messages.
   b. No, thanks. I'll call back later.
   c. Yes, I left a message.

2. a. Please leave me a message, and I'll call you back.
   b. Would you like to leave a message?
   c. May I ask who's calling?

3. a. When is a good time to call?
   b. OK, I'll return your call.
   c. Thanks, I will.

4. a. No, he sent me a text message.
   b. He can't come to class today.
   c. I don't know. He hung up.

5. a. Are you screening your calls?
   b. Check your text messages.
   c. Hang up and call me back.

6. a. You can make a call.
   b. Don't forget to silence your phone.
   c. Can I borrow your phone?

E 🔊 **Check predictions.** Listen and check your answers. **Track 24**

F 🔁 What does the voicemail greeting on your cell phone say? Say it to a partner in English.

4 SPEAKING

A 🔊 Celia and Lisa are chatting when their phone call is interrupted. Listen to the conversations. Which one is more formal? **Track 25**

LISA:	Hello?
CELIA:	Lisa? Hi. It's Celia.
LISA:	Oh, hey, Celia. How are you doing?
CELIA:	Pretty good. So, are you ready for the big test tomorrow?
LISA:	Almost, but I have one question... (phone beeps) Oh, Celia... can you hang on? I've got another call coming in.
CELIA:	Yeah, no problem.
LISA:	Hello?
PROF. LARSON:	Yes, hello. May I speak to Lisa Sanchez, please?

LISA:	Speaking.
PROF. LARSON:	Lisa, this is Professor Larson. You left me a message earlier today. You had a question about tomorrow's exam.
LISA:	Oh, right. Professor Larson, could you hold for a moment?
PROF. LARSON:	Of course.
LISA:	Hello, Celia? Can I call you back? I have to take the other call.
CELIA:	Sure. Talk to you later.

B 👥 Practice the conversation in **A** with two classmates. Use your own names in the conversation.

SPEAKING STRATEGY

C 🔄 Make the conversation below more formal by changing the underlined words. Use the Useful Expressions to help you. Then practice it with a partner.

A: Hello?

B: <u>Hi. Is Kurt there?</u> _____

A: <u>Who's calling?</u> _____

B: This is Martin.

A: OK, <u>hang on.</u> _____

B: Sure.

A: Sorry, he's not in. <u>Can I take a message?</u> _____

B: No, thanks. I'll call back later.

D 🔄 Create two phone conversations with your partner. One should be informal. The other should be more formal.

Useful Expressions	
Using the Telephone	
Asking for someone and responding	Hi, Lisa? / Hi. Is Lisa there?
	Hello. May / Could / Can I speak to Lisa, please? [formal]
	This is Lisa. / Speaking.
Asking for identification of caller	Who's calling?
	May I ask who's calling? [formal]
Asking someone to wait	Hang on. / Can you hang on (for a moment / second)?
	Would / Could you hold (for a moment / second)? [formal]
Taking a message	Can I take a message?
	May I take a message? [formal]
	Would you like to leave a message? [formal]

E 👥 Perform your conversations for another pair. Can they guess which one is more formal?

5 GRAMMAR

A Turn to pages 76–77. Complete the exercises. Then do **B–D** below.

Asking for Permission						Responses
Would	it be OK	if	I	used	your phone?	Certainly. / Of course. / Sure, no problem. (I'm) sorry, but…
Would	you mind					No, not at all. / No, go ahead. (I'm) sorry, but…
Do	you mind	if	I	use	your phone?	No, not at all. / No, go ahead. (I'm) sorry, but…
May / Could / Can			I	use	your phone?	Certainly. / Of course. / Sure, no problem. (I'm) sorry, but…

B Look at the photo. The passenger is asking the flight attendant for permission. Use the words in parentheses to complete the questions.

1. (move to another seat)

   Would you _____?

2. (have a vegetarian meal)

   May _____?

3. (use the restroom now)

   Would it _____?

4. (turn on my laptop now)

   Can _____?

C Read each situation. Use the verbs in parentheses to ask permission.

1. Your friend is doing his or her homework. You have finished your homework, and you want to watch TV. Ask permission informally. (turn on)

   _____

2. You're invited to a party on Saturday night. You want your friend to go, too. Ask the host's permission a little formally. (bring)

   _____

3. You were sick yesterday and missed an important test in class. You want to take it this Friday. Ask your instructor's permission formally. (take)

   _____

4. Your instructor doesn't allow phones in class. You are waiting for an important text and need to leave your phone on silent. Ask your instructor's permission formally. (check)

   _____

D 🔄 With a partner, take turns asking and answering the questions in **C**. Refuse (say *no* to) one request and give a reason why.

6 COMMUNICATION

A Get into groups of three: Student A, Student B, and Student C. Read the instructions.

Student A: Choose one piece of good news from the list below.

☐ I bought a new car! ☐ I got an "A" on my exam! ☐ I've got two tickets to a concert!

☐ I found your lost wallet! ☐ I got a new job! ☐ your idea: _____

Student B: Have a piece of paper and a pen ready to write down a message.

Student C: Choose a reason you are busy from the list below.

☐ You're taking a nap. ☐ You're out with friends.

☐ You're at the library. ☐ your idea: _____

B Work with your group. Follow the steps below.

Step 1: Student A has some good news for Student C, but Student B answers the phone. Student B explains why Student C is busy and takes Student A's message.

A: Hello. May I speak to Bianca, please?

B: I'm sorry, she's taking a nap. Can I take a message?

A: Yes. This is Ernesto. Would you tell her I found her wallet?

B: Sure, no problem. What's your number?

A: It's...

Step 2: Student B writes down the message and gives the information to Student C.

● :: WHILE YOU WERE OUT :: ●

Ernesto called.

Time: _3:30_

Message: _He found your wallet._

Phone number: _555-9733_

> **Remember! How to make a request**
> **Can / Could / Will / Would** you answer the phone?
> OK. / Sure, no problem. / I'd be glad to.
> **Would you mind** answer<u>ing</u> the phone?
> No, not at all. / No, I'd be glad to.

Step 3: Student C calls Student A back to find out about the good news. Ask at least two questions.

C: Hi, Ernesto. It's Bianca.

A: Hi, Bianca. I have some good news. I found your wallet.

C: That's great! Where did you find it?

A: In the school cafeteria.

C: Thanks a lot, Ernesto. Could you bring it to school tomorrow?

C Switch roles so everyone gets a chance to play each role.

It is polite to step aside if you need to use your phone in a busy place.

1 VOCABULARY

A Read the quiz. Pay attention to the words in **blue**. Use your dictionary to help you. Talk about the meanings of the words with a partner. Then complete the chart with a word or phrase in **blue**.

Word	Opposite
add / post	delete
ban	
polite	
raise your voice	
respond	ignore
thoughtless	
turn down (the music)	
turn down (a request)	

> If you *respond* to a question, you answer it. The opposite is *ignore*.

B Take the quiz. Check (✓) your answers.

C Explain your answers in **B** to a partner.

Phone Etiquette: How polite are you?

1. You're on a date. You get a text from a friend. What do you do?
   - ☐ Check it and **respond** right away.
   - ☐ **Ignore** the message. Answering it now would be **rude**.
   - ☐ My idea: _____

2. The person next to you on the bus is listening to loud music. What do you do?
   - ☐ Ask him to **turn down** the music. You don't want to hear it!
   - ☐ Put on your headphones and **turn up** your music loud, too.
   - ☐ My idea: _____

3. I think we should...
   - ☐ **ban** phones in crowded places like subways and airplanes. No one should be able to use them.
   - ☐ **allow** phones everywhere. I should always be able to use my phone.
   - ☐ My idea: _____

4. When talking on my phone in public, I usually...
   - ☐ **raise my voice** so the caller can hear me clearly.
   - ☐ **lower my voice**. I don't want others to hear my conversation.
   - ☐ My idea: _____

5. You want to post some funny photos of your friend online, but the photos might be embarrassing. What do you do?
   - ☐ Show your friend the photos first. It's the **thoughtful** thing to do.
   - ☐ Post the photos. If he doesn't like them, you can **delete** them.
   - ☐ My idea: _____

6. You just started a new job, and your boss sends you a friend request on social media. What do you do?
   - ☐ **Accept** the request. He must like me!
   - ☐ **Turn down** the request. I don't want people at work seeing my personal information.
   - ☐ My idea: _____

2 LISTENING

A 🔊 **Listen for gist.** Read the sentences below. Then listen to three different conversations and choose the best answer for each sentence. **Track 26**

Conversation 1

1. The speakers are in a _____.

   a. classroom   b. restaurant   c. movie theater

Conversation 2

2. The speakers are _____ a party.

   a. taking photos at   b. posting pictures from   c. looking at photos from

Conversation 3

3. The speakers are waiting for their friend Manny. Manny is _____.

   a. late for a party   b. still at school   c. talking on his phone

B 🔊 **Listen for details; Infer information.** Listen again and choose the best answer. **Track 26**

Conversation 1

1. The man is asking the girl to _____.

   a. turn off her phone   b. lower her voice   c. turn down her music

2. The girl _____.

   a. apologizes and agrees   b. ignores the man   c. gets angry with the man

Conversation 2

3. The girl thinks the photo of her is _____.

   a. thoughtful   b. silly   c. terrible

4. The girl decides to _____.

   a. ignore people's comments   b. tell Connor to delete the photos   c. both a and b

Conversation 3

5. The guy texts Manny, and Manny _____.

   a. responds right away   b. ignores the text   c. calls the guy

6. The girl thinks Manny is _____.

   a. polite   b. angry   c. thoughtless

C 🗣 Answer the questions with a partner.

1. In each conversation, what happened? Use your answers in **A** and **B** to help you explain.

2. Have any of these things ever happened to you?

> In the first conversation, the girl was... and the man asked her to...

PHONE-FREE ON THE ROAD?

3 READING 🔊 Track 27

A 🔄 **Read for the gist.** Read the title and first paragraph on the next page. Tell a partner: What does the new law do?

B **Read for opinions.** Read the article. Then complete the sentences below. Why does each person have this opinion about cell phones and driving? Write a reason.

1. Simon thinks some / all cell phone use should be allowed / banned.
   Reason: _____
   _____

2. Alexis thinks some / all cell phone use should be allowed / banned.
   Reason: _____
   _____

3. Ann thinks some / all cell phone use should be allowed / banned.
   Reason: _____
   _____

C **Infer meaning.** Find these expressions in the reading:

come on, I mean, look

Match each expression with its meaning.

Use this expression to…

1. say you disagree with something
   _____

2. make something you've just said clearer _____

3. introduce an important point
   _____

D 🔷 **Summarize and evaluate; Exemplify.** Work in a group of three. Follow the steps below.

1. Each person should take one person's comment and read it aloud. Try to read with feeling.

2. Role-play a conversation among the three people. Talk about the law and your opinion about it. Try to make the others agree with you.

3. Whose opinion(s) from the reading do you agree with? Why?

A new law bans all cell phone use while you are driving—including talking on the phone and texting. The fine[1] for breaking the law[2] is high, but many drivers are ignoring the ban. What do you think about this problem?

Simon R. Peru

Look, I've got a phone, and I'm glad to have it. But come on! Talking on the phone, checking social media, or texting while you're driving is crazy. And yet, I see people doing things like this every day. Using your phone and driving at the same time causes accidents. There have been many studies to prove this. My question is, where are the police? They don't seem to care, so it's easy for drivers to ignore the law. When people are afraid of getting a large fine, phone use in the car will stop. Everyone needs to learn that when you drive, you should turn off your phone. It's very simple!

Alexis C. Greece

Ok, I agree—texting while driving is hazardous. But can we really ban all phone use in cars? For example, yesterday I was driving home, and I saw an accident on the road. I called and reported it. Did I stop driving to make the call? No. But did I help someone? Yes. We need to talk more about this new law. I just don't think the answer to the problem is so simple.

Ann T. China

I don't think we can ban all phone use in cars—especially if you use a hands-free device[3] while driving, like I do. Sometimes my friend is in the car with me. I talk to her while I'm driving. Isn't that dangerous? I mean, isn't talking on the phone the same as talking to a passenger? In my opinion, they are the same, and so I think we should be able to chat on the phone while we're driving.

[1] A *fine* is money you pay when you break a law.

[2] If you *break a law*, you do something illegal.

[3] A *hands-free device* allows you to use your phone in the car without touching it or looking at it.

4 GRAMMAR

A Turn to pages 77–78. Complete the exercises. Then do **B** and **C** below.

Verb + Infinitive vs. Verb + Gerund	
I **need** <u>to buy</u> a new phone.	Certain verbs can be followed by an <u>infinitive</u>: *agree, decide, hope, learn, need, plan, seem, want, would like*
I **avoid** <u>talking</u> on the phone when I'm driving.	Certain verbs can be followed by a <u>gerund</u>: *appreciate, avoid, dislike, enjoy, feel like, keep, (not) mind*
I **tried** <u>to call</u> / <u>calling</u> you earlier.	Certain verbs can be followed by an infinitive or a gerund: *begin, can't stand, hate, like, love, prefer, start, try*

B How do you feel about the activities below? Write sentences in your notebook, using the verbs in the box.

avoid	can't stand / hate	enjoy	like	(not) mind	need	prefer

Example: <u>I hate talking on the phone. I prefer to text people.</u>

1. talk on the phone
2. respond to texts late at night
3. walk and text at the same time
4. take selfies in public

5. post weird photos of myself online
6. say mean things on social media
7. play games on my phone
8. accept friend requests from strangers online

C Work in a small group. Compare your answers in **B**.

> I can't stand when people take selfies in public.

> Really? I think it's fun.

5 WRITING

A 🔄 Read the question and the paragraph. Then discuss with a partner: What is the writer's response? What examples does she give to explain her response?

B List all the ways you use your phone in a day. Then use your notes and the example to write a paragraph that answers the question. Use at least two verbs from the grammar chart.

C 🔄 Exchange papers with a partner.

1. Answer the questions in the direction line in **A**. Circle any mistakes in your partner's paper.

2. Return the paper to your partner. Make corrections to your own paragraph.

3. Are you and your partner similar or different? Why do you think people spend so much time on their phones?

Question: *Do you spend a lot of time on your phone? Why or why not?*

Yes, I spend a lot of time on my phone. For example, when I wake up, I check my phone and I respond to texts right away. Then I check social media. When I have breakfast, I can't stand just eating. I prefer to watch a video or play a game. Even at the bus stop, I dislike just waiting. I usually call a friend or browse the Internet. At night, I avoid doing my homework by using my phone. I text my friends or listen to music. My mom tried to ban phones from 7:00 to 10:00 PM in our house, but it didn't work. We are all addicted to our phones!

6 COMMUNICATION

A 👥 Work in a group of four. Felipe is 11 years old. He wants a phone. Each group member should choose one person below. Read <u>only</u> the information for your part.

Word Bank

If you are *addicted* to something, you can't stop doing it.

Felipe Dias

Mrs. Dias

Mr. Dias

Felipe's school principal

I want to get a phone. All my friends have one. I need one to text my friends, watch videos, and play games. And without a phone, I don't know what my friends are doing.

I don't mind getting Felipe a phone. He has so many after-school activities, and I worry about him. I can't stand wondering where he is. I want to be able to text or call him if I have to.

I've avoided getting Felipe a phone. I know he wants one, but I'd prefer to wait another year. Do you know how many adults are addicted to their phones? I mean, at his age, Felipe should be playing sports, not staring at a screen.

Cell phones are convenient, but too much phone use can be bad for children's brains. Also, there are lots of problems these days with Internet bullying at school, and phones make this easy. Texting in class is also a problem. I don't think kids should bring phones to school.

B 👥 Role-play a discussion among the four people. Each person should explain his or her opinion. Bring in your own ideas, too. Try to make the other people agree with you.

C 👥 Should Felipe get a phone? Why or why not? What is your group's final decision? Tell the class.

> Come on, Dad. I need a phone. All my friends have one!

> Look, Felipe, you don't need to have a cell phone.

1 STORYBOARD

A Harry is telling Linda about his dream. Complete the story. For some blanks, more than one answer is possible.

B Cover the story. Take turns telling it to your partner.

2 SEE IT AND SAY IT

A Yesterday there was a movie premiere at the Galaxy Theater. Look at the picture. What were the people doing when the movie star arrived? Tell your partner.

B Think of a movie you know. Write the name of the movie on the sign in the picture. Invite your partner to the premiere. Your partner should ask one or two questions.

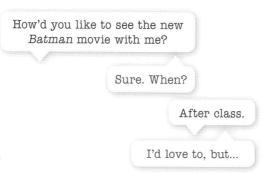

How'd you like to see the new *Batman* movie with me?

Sure. When?

After class.

I'd love to, but...

C Invite other friends to see the movie. Practice inviting and accepting or refusing invitations.

3 LISTENING

A 🔊 Read the information in the box. Then listen and complete each person's profile below. Use one word in each blank. **Track 28**

> Every year, the Dream Big Foundation gives $10,000 to a person between the ages of 17 and 22 so that he or she can do something important—go to college, study abroad, start a business, and so on. This year, the foundation received thousands of applications from all over the world. There are now two finalists—Teresa Silva and Daniel Okoye. Who should get the prize?

Name: Teresa Silva   **Age:** 21

What she does:

- She created a _____ to help poor artists sell their products to the _____.

- When a product sells, she takes _____ percent and gives _____ percent to the artists.

- Since _____, she has already sold _____ items.

Why she needs the money:

- There's a lot of _____ to do.

What she plans to do with the money:

- She plans to _____ one more person.

- She hopes to sell _____ as many items.

Name: Daniel Okoye   **Age:** 18

What he does:

- He's a _____.

- He's from _____, but he moved to _____ when he was eleven.

Why he needs the money:

- His parents _____ when he was _____.

- He has no money for _____.

What he plans to do with the money:

- He wants to study _____.

- He hopes to become a _____ and help others.

B You work for the Dream Big Foundation. Review your notes in **A**. Answer the questions.

1. Which words in the box below would you use to describe Teresa and Daniel? Why?

2. In your opinion, which person should win the money? Why? Give at least two reasons.

courageous	cautious	clever	efficient	flexible
ambitious	careless	independent	pleasant	punctual

C 👥 Get into a group of three or four people. Compare your answers in **B**. Together choose the winner of this year's prize. Then share your answer with the class.

> I think Teresa should get the money because she's very clever.

> So do I.

> Yeah, but Daniel lost his parents as a teenager and...

4 SPOT THE ERRORS

A Find and correct the mistake(s) in the sentences. You have five minutes.

1. A: I really liked that movie.
   B: So am I.

2. After graduation, I hope visit my cousin in New York City.

3. Sorry I missed your call. I watched TV, and I didn't hear the phone.

4. You seem quietly today. Are you OK?

5. Maya's worked for the same company since two years. Now she wants quit and get a new job.

6. A: How long you know John?
   B: Since high school. We are friends for many years.

B ✪ Compare your answers in **A** with a partner's. If you have different answers, explain your corrections.

5 SPEAK FOR A MINUTE!

A Read the questions and think about your answers. Do not tell anyone your answers.

1. Talk about the last movie you saw. What was the story about?

2. Talk about a festival or holiday that you know. Where and when does it take place? What happens?

3. Which would you prefer to do—work for a company or work for yourself? Why?

4. Talk about the last party you went to. What was it for? Who hosted it? Did you have a good time? Why or why not?

5. To speak English well, what do you need to do? What should you try not to do?

6. Name something you've wanted to do for a long time. Why haven't you done it yet?

B ♧ Get into a group of four people. Follow the steps below.

1. On six small pieces of paper, write the numbers 1 to 6 (for questions 1–6 in **A**). Put the six numbers in a hat or bag.

2. One person picks a number out of the hat or bag and answers that question in **A**.

3. If the person can talk for one minute without stopping, he or she gets one point. Then put the number back in the bag.

4. Then it's another person's turn. Repeat steps 2 and 3. Continue playing for 20 minutes. The winner is the person with the most points.

 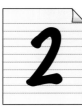    

6 STORYBOARD

A Pia is calling Bob, her boss, at work. Complete the conversations. For some blanks, more than one answer is possible.

B 🔗 In groups of three, practice the conversations. Then change roles and practice again.

C 🔗 Think of an interesting place to make a telephone call from. Then make your own conversation like the one above. Practice with your group.

7 SEE IT AND SAY IT

A Look at the picture of Leo's house. He went on a trip, but he forgot to do many things before he left. On a piece of paper, make a list of what he forgot to do.

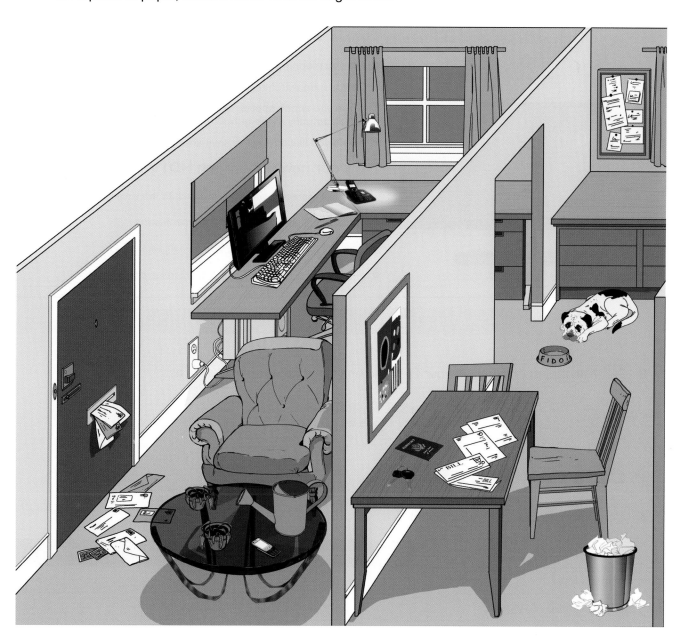

B Work with a partner. Pretend that you are Leo and call a friend. Choose three things you forgot to do and ask for help. Then switch roles.

> I don't remember turning off the light in the living room. Can you do it for me?

> Sure. No problem.

8 A TV AD

A  Read the ad. Circle the correct answer(s) in the sentences. Then unscramble the adjectives. Check your answers with a partner.

This Week's Best Buy!

50 in / 127 cm

★ **Are you planning** buying / to buy **a new TV?**

★ **Do you hate** watching / to watch **movies on a small screen?**

★ **When you watch sports, do you want** feeling / to feel **like you're actually at the game?**

★ **Would you like** saving / to save **energy when you watch TV?**

Try our new flat screen HDTV!

And you'll appreciate watching / to watch **TV in a whole new way!**

★ (beerraakml) _____ picture quality!

★ (fabfadrole) _____ -Now only $900!

★ (dealurb) _____ -Guaranteed to last 20 years!

B With a partner, compare your TV to the one in the ad using *(not) as… as.*

> My TV isn't as expensive as the TV in the ad.

9 OLD FAVORITES

A Complete the chart with your favorites.

	When you were younger	Now
Snack food		
Music group or singer		
Piece of clothing you own(ed)		
Hobby		
Weekend activities		

B With a partner, ask and answer questions about your present and past favorites. Use *used to* for the past favorites. Have you changed a lot?

> What snack food did you use to eat?

> I used to eat a lot of sweets, but these days, I eat healthier snacks.

10 FIRST TRIP

A Emma Goldstein is 90 years old. She took her first trip on an airplane last month. Read what she said. Then correct the mistake(s) in each sentence. They can be mistakes in grammar or vocabulary. Some sentences can be fixed more than one way.

1. I used to ~~was~~ *be* afraid of flying.

2. Last month, I made a call from my daughter.

3. She said, "You must to pack your bags. We're taking a trip."

4. I didn't want to going at first because I disliked to fly.

5. I took two pieces of boarding passes on the plane.

6. The flight attendant was nice. She helped me put everything in the oxygen mask.

7. Airplane travel is not as scarier as I thought.

8. I can now proudly say, "I have flying on an airplane!"

B Ask your partner about a trip he or she has taken.

11 LISTENING

A Read the phone messages below. Then listen and circle the correct answer for each question. **Track 29**

1. Which message did Sheila leave for Tom?

WHILE YOU WERE OUT	WHILE YOU WERE OUT	WHILE YOU WERE OUT
Sheila called. She wants to meet soon. She will call again at 5:00.	Sheila called. She can't meet tomorrow. Please call her.	Sheila called. She can't meet today. She wants to meet tomorrow at 2:00.

2. Which message did Ted leave for Penny's brother?

WHILE YOU WERE OUT	WHILE YOU WERE OUT	WHILE YOU WERE OUT
Ted called. His computer crashed and won't start. He wants you to fix it. Can you call him? His number is 555-9083.	Ted called. He has a question about his new laptop. Please call him back.	Ted called. He wants you to help him buy a new computer. He'll call you later.

UNIT 1 GOALS

LESSON A

Vocabulary

apply → application
compete → competition
consider → consideration
decide → decision
observe → observation
recommend → recommendation

Speaking Strategy

Responding to bad news
(I'm) sorry to hear that.
That's too bad.
How disappointing.
You must be disappointed.

Offering to help
If you want to talk, (just) call me.
If there's anything I can do, (just)
   let me know.

LESSON B

Vocabulary

be (your) own boss
a catch
create a résumé
do an internship
go back to school
mentor
opportunity
take a risk / take risks
take (time) off
(a school) term

Talking about indefinite *future time*
at some point
in a few (days, weeks)
soon
in the near future
someday / eventually

UNIT 2 STORYTELLING

LESSON A

Vocabulary

a **character** in a story
based on
the beginning / end of a story
easy ↔ **hard to follow**
fantasy
heartbreaking
heartwarming
(happy) ending
made-up (land)
make up a story
series
**The story is about… / It tells
   the story of…**
tell a story
true
(un)predictable
(un)realistic
uplifting
violent

Speaking Strategy

Keeping a story going
One day,…
So, (then),…
Later,…
After that,…
As it turns out,…
It turns out that,…

LESSON B

Vocabulary

arrogant
clever
discover (+ *that* + sentence)
eloquent
incredible
overcome (a problem)
patient
quick ↔ slow
struggle (to do something)
survive

UNIT 3 TECHNOLOGY

LESSON A

Vocabulary

affordable
dependable
durable
fad
fashionable
features
flash in the pan
manageable
portable
practical
product
reliable
remarkable

Speaking Strategy

Offering a counterargument
Stating what other people think
A lot of people say (that)…
Some people think (that) (she's
    really shy).

Explaining what you think
(But,) actually,…
(But,) in fact, / in reality,…
(But,) the truth / fact / reality is
    (she's very outgoing).

LESSON B

Vocabulary

consume
have a(n) (positive / negative)
    effect
located
prevent
recycle
reduce
rescue
restore
transform

UNIT 4 TELEPHONING

LESSON A

Vocabulary

Phrases with *phone*
answer the phone ↔ **hang up**
    the phone
be on the phone / **talk on the**
    phone
borrow / **use someone's phone**
mute / **silence your phone**
turn on your phone ↔ **turn off**
    your phone

Phrases with *call*
call someone / **make a call**
call someone back / **return**
    a call
get a call from someone
screen your calls

Phrases with *message*
check your (text / phone)
    messages
get a (text / phone) message ↔
    leave a message / **send a**
    message
take a message

Speaking Strategy

Using the telephone
Asking for someone and
    responding
Hi, Lisa? / Hi. Is Lisa there?
Hello. May / Could / Can I speak
    to Lisa, please? [formal]
This is Lisa. / Speaking.

Asking for identification of caller
Who's calling?
May I ask who's calling? [formal]

Asking someone to wait
Hang on. / Can you hang on (for a
    moment / second)?
Would / Could you hold (for a
    moment / second)? [formal]

Taking a message
Can I take a message?
May I take a message? [formal]
Would you like to leave a
    message? [formal]

LESSON B

Vocabulary

add / **post** ↔ **delete**
(be) addicted (to something)
at the last minute
ban ↔ **allow**
bullying
polite ↔ **rude**
raise your voice ↔ **lower your**
    voice
respond ↔ **ignore**
thoughtless ↔ **thoughtful**
turn down (the music) ↔ **turn**
    up (the music)
turn down (a request) ↔ **accept**
    (a request)

Come on.
I mean…
Look…

UNIT 1 GOALS

LESSON A

Plans and Decisions with *be going* to and *will*			
I'm / You're / He's / She's / We're / They're	(not)		**going to** go to Harvard.
Maybe	I / you / he / she / we / they	**will** won't	see a movie.

Contractions (*is / are*)
you're not = you aren't
she's not = she isn't

Contractions (*will*)
I'll / you'll / he'll / she'll / we'll / they'll

Use *be going to* to talk about future plans you have already made. (You thought about the plans beforehand.) *Good news! I'm going to attend Harvard in the fall.*

Use *will* for future events when you make a sudden decision at the time of speaking. (You didn't think about the plans beforehand.) *I don't have any plans tonight. Maybe I'll see a movie.*

A Complete the statements and questions with the correct form of *be going to*. Some items have more than one answer.

1. _____ (I / not) learn English in another country.

2. _____ (you) join a club on campus?

3. _____ (she) decide on a college soon.

4. _____ (they / not) pass the test.

5. _____ (she) take attendance?

6. _____ (we) live in a dorm room.

7. _____ (he / not) attend a private school.

8. _____ (they) finish their homework?

B Complete the sentences with the correct form of *be going to* or *will*.

1. I graduate from high school in June. Then I _____ attend college in the fall.

2. I'm bored and don't know what to do. Wait, I know... I _____ call my friend.

3. WAITER: What would you like today?

   CUSTOMER: Let's see... I _____ have the chicken and rice, please.

4. I bought my ticket last month. I _____ visit Paris from July 1 to July 14.

5. A: This box is too heavy!
   B: Wait! I _____ help you.

6. I _____ apply to three schools.

LESSON B

Predictions with *be going to* and *will*	
She's **going to** / **will** be very successful. Some students **aren't going to** / **won't** pass the exam.	You can use *be going to* and *will* to make predictions (guesses) about the future.
He'll definitely / probably study business in college. Maybe he'll study business in college. He definitely / probably **won't** study history.	You can use *definitely*, *probably*, or *maybe* to say how certain you are about something. Notice how they are used with *will* and be *going to*. *Definitely:* You are 100% certain of something.
She's definitely / probably **going to** attend college in the fall. Maybe she's **going to** get a job after graduation. She definitely / probably **isn't going to** go to college. / She's definitely / probably **not going to** go to college.	*Probably:* You are very certain of something. *Maybe:* You think something is possible.
A: **Is** she **going to go** to graduate school? B: Maybe. I'm not sure. A: **Will** she go to graduate school? B: Probably not. I think she wants to get a job.	You can ask a *Yes / No* prediction question with *be going to* or *will*. It's common to answer these questions with only *definitely*, *probably*, or *maybe*. To express the negative, add *not* after *definitely*, *probably*, or *maybe*.

A Answer each question with the words in parentheses and *be going to* or *will*. Some items may have more than one possible answer.

1. A: What are Mario's plans for next year?

   B: I'm not sure. _____ (he / go back to school / maybe).

2. A: Are Clara and Tony going to get married?

   B: Yeah, _____ (they / get married / definitely / someday).

3. A: Is Rob going to go to the school party tonight?

   B: _____ (not / go / probably / he). He's sick.

4. A: Jun applied to Seoul National University. It's hard to get accepted.

   B: I know, but _____ (get accepted / definitely / he). He's smart.

5. A: Where's the bus? It's late.

   B: _____ (probably / not / be / it) here for a while. Traffic is bad.

6. A: Is it going to rain tomorrow?

   B: Yeah, _____ (rain / it / probably) tomorrow, too.

B 🔁 Ask and answer the questions in **A** with a partner. In which dialogs can you use a short answer with *definitely*, *probably*, or *maybe*? Say them again with a partner.

UNIT **2** STORYTELLING

LESSON A

The Past Continuous Tense: Statements				
Subject	*was / were (not)*	**Verb + *ing***		
I He / She	was / wasn't	**studying**	English	at four o'clock. last summer. after lunchtime.
You We They	were / weren't			

Use the past continuous tense to talk about an action <u>in progress</u> in the past. The action can happen at a specific point in time or over a period of time.

We don't usually use the past continuous with stative verbs (*hear, need, know*, etc.).

Use the simple past, not the past continuous, to talk about a <u>completed</u> action:

>   A: *I called you last night.*   B: *I <u>didn't hear</u> my phone. I <u>was watching</u> TV.*

You can use the past continuous with the simple past to show that one action was in progress when another action happened. Notice the use of *when*:

>   *I <u>was taking</u> a shower when the phone <u>rang</u>.*

The Past Continuous Tense: Questions						
	***Wh-* word**	***was / were***	**Subject**	**Verb + *ing***		**Answers**
Yes / No questions		Were	you they	**reading**	a story?	Yes, I was. / No, I wasn't. Yes, they were. / No, they weren't.
		Was	she			Yes, she was. / No, she wasn't.
Wh- questions	What	were	you they	**reading?**		(I was reading) (They were reading) a story.
		was	he			(He was reading) a story.

A Read the story. Find the eight grammar errors and correct them.

Last summer, I'm eating dinner in a restaurant with two friends. We were talking and laughing when I was noticing a woman coming in. It was very hot outside, but the woman was wearing a heavy winter coat. The restaurant was nearly empty, but she was sitting next to our table anyway. The woman was looking at me for a second and gave me a friendly smile. After that, I forgot about her.

Later on, we was paying our bill and getting ready to go home when one of my friends was realizing that his wallet was missing from his back pocket. We were calling the police, and they came right away. Unfortunately, I wasn't seeing anything, so I couldn't help very much. As it turned out, the police knew the woman and were looking for her. They never found her, and my friend never got his money back.

B Complete the sentences with the past continuous or simple past form of the verb.

1. They (have) _____ a good time when the woman (come) _____ in.

2. The woman (give) _____ a friendly smile when she (sit) _____ down.

3. They (notice) _____ the wallet was missing when they (pay) _____ the bill.

4. They (call) _____ the police when they (notice) _____ the theft.

5. They told the police they (see / not) _____ anything when the woman (take) _____ the wallet.

LESSON B

Adverbs of Manner	
Cinderella smiled **shyly** at the prince.	**Adverbs of manner** describe how something is done. Many end in -*ly*, and they often come after a verb.
He opened <u>the door</u> **quietly**. She answered <u>the question</u> **correctly**. *Not: He opened quietly the door.* ~~*She answered correctly the question.*~~	When there is <u>an object</u> (a noun or pronoun) after the verb, the adverb usually comes at the end of the sentence.
She was <u>different</u> from other children. You seem <u>unhappy</u>.	Remember: <u>Adjectives</u>, not adverbs, come after stative verbs (words like *be*, *have*, *hear*, *need*, *know*, *seem*).
She drives too **fast**. He studied **hard** for the exam. They didn't do **well** in school.	Some common adverbs of manner don't end in -*ly*. Some examples are: *fast*, *hard*, and *well*.

A Rewrite each sentence using the adverb form of the word in parentheses. Use a different verb if necessary.

1. He is fluent in three languages. (fluent)

   <u>He speaks three languages fluently.</u>

2. In the famous story, the hare is a fast runner, and the tortoise is a slow walker. (quick, slow)

   _____

3. In the movie *Star Wars*, Luke Skywalker is a brave fighter. (brave)

   _____

4. When she left the party, Cinderella lost a shoe. (accident)

   _____

5. In the story, the man disappears in a mysterious way. (mysterious)

   _____

6. The girl is only six, but she is a very good singer. (good)

   _____

B In five minutes, how many sentences can you make with the words below? Time yourself. You can use present or past forms of the verbs. Compare your answers with a partner's.

boy	girl	dragon	song
fight	run	sing	struggle with
beautifully	bravely	fast / quickly	slowly

> The boy and girl fought the dragon bravely.

UNIT 3 TECHNOLOGY

LESSON A

Used to			
Subject	**use(d) to**	**Verb**	
I	**used to**	wear	glasses.
We	didn't **use to**	own	a computer.

Use *used to* for habits and actions that happened during a period of time in the past but are no longer happening now: *I used to wear glasses, but now I wear contacts.*

Use a time expression like *now* or *today* to make a contrast between the present and the past:
We didn't use to own a computer, but <u>now</u> *we have three of them at home.*

Expressions like *nowadays* and *these days* can be used for people or events "in general":
People used to use their phones only for making calls. These days, they use them to do lots of things.

Notice the spelling of *use to* in negative statements.

Did	**Subject**	*use to*	**Verb**		**Responses**
Did	you	**use to**	wear	glasses?	Yes, I did. / No, I didn't.
	she		own	a computer?	Yes, she did. / No, she didn't.

Notice the spelling of *use to* in questions.

A Complete the sentences about *used to*.

1. Use *used to* to talk about the   a. present.   b. past.

2. *Used to* is followed by   a. the base form of a verb.   b. a gerund (*ing* form).

3. Use *use to* in negative statements and   a. responses.   b. questions.

B Write sentences to compare life today with life 100 years ago. Use the time expressions given. Follow the model.

1. People had bigger families. (nowadays)

   People used to have bigger families. Nowadays families are smaller.

2. Not many people owned a television. (today)

   _____

3. Not many women worked outside of the home. (now)

   _____

4. Telephones weren't portable. (these days)

   _____

5. Technology wasn't affordable. (now)

   _____

6. People read books instead of watching TV. (today)

   _____

LESSON B

Comparisons with *as... as*	

Phone A is 12 cm. Phone B is 12 cm.
   Phone A is **as** <u>big</u> **as** phone B.
 	
Phone A costs $100. Phone B costs $100.
   Phone A costs **as** <u>much</u> **as** phone B.
	Use *as* + adjective / adverb + *as* to show that two things are equal.

Camera A isn't **as** <u>affordable</u> **as** Camera B. Maria didn't do **as** <u>well</u> **as** Carlos on the test.	You can use *not as...* as to show that things are not equal.
My phone works **as** well **as** <u>your phone</u>. = My phone works **as** well **as** <u>yours</u>. I like this phone **as** much **as** that <u>phone</u>. = I like this phone **as** much **as** that <u>one</u>. She studies **as** hard **as** <u>he studies</u>. (not common) She studies **as** hard **as** <u>he does</u>. (common) She studies **as** hard **as** <u>him</u>.	Sometimes after *as... as*, you can end a sentence with a pronoun. In spoken and written English, it's common not to repeat the main verb after *as... as*, but to say things as shown in the example.

A   Unscramble the sentences.

1. speaks / She / as / you / English / do / well / as

   _____

2. us / don't / as / have / many / You / classes / as

   _____

3. computer / heavy / as / This / isn't / as / one / that

   _____

4. My / durable / as / tablet / as / isn't / yours

   _____

5. jacket / as / That / is / this / one / as / fashionable

   _____

B Compare the two vacuum cleaners in the chart by completing the sentences with *(not) as… as*. There may be more than one possible correct answer.

	The Vacuum Star	**The Vacuum Pro**
weight	6 kilos	6 kilos
price	$450	$150
durability	lasts 5–10 years	lasts 4–5 years
popularity	☆☆☆	☆☆☆☆☆
convenience	Robotic; cleans everywhere by itself	Robotic; cleans everywhere by itself

1. weight

   The Vacuum Star _____weighs as much as_____ the Vacuum Pro. / The Vacuum Star _____is as heavy as_____ the Vacuum Pro.

2. price

   The Vacuum Pro _____ the Vacuum Star.

3. durability

   The Vacuum Pro _____ the Vacuum Star.

4. popularity

   The Vacuum Star _____ the Vacuum Pro.

5. convenience

   The Vacuum Star _____ the Vacuum Pro.

LESSON A

Asking for Permission							Responses
❶	**Would**	it be OK	if	I	used	your phone?	Certainly. / Of course. / Sure, no problem. (I'm) sorry, but…
❷	**Would**	you mind					No, not at all. / No, go ahead. (I'm) sorry, but…
❸	**Do**	you mind	if	I	use	your phone?	No, not at all. / No, go ahead. (I'm) sorry, but…
❹	**May / Could / Can**			I	use	your phone?	Certainly. / Of course. / Sure, no problem. (I'm) sorry, but…

❶ & ❷ The use of the past tense verb (e.g., *used*) makes requests with *Would* sound slightly more polite or formal.

❷ & ❸ To agree to a request made with *Would you mind / Do you mind*, answer with *no* (e.g., *No, I don't mind. You can use my phone.*)

❹ *May I* and *Could I* are slightly more formal than *Can I.*

A Unscramble the words to make questions.

1. you / I / messages / would / my / if / text / mind / checked

   _____

2. him / a / leave / could / message / I

   _____

3. OK / turned / it / phone / be / on / would / I / my / if

   _____

4. make / can / a / call / home / phone / I / quick

   _____

B 🔁 Complete the dialogs. Then practice them with a partner.

1. A: _____ _____ mind if I opened the window?

   B: _____, not _____ _____. It's really hot in here.

2. A: May _____ _____ here?

   B: _____ _____, but my friend is sitting there.

3. A: _____ _____ mind if I turn up the volume a bit? It's hard to hear.

   B: _____, _____ ahead.

4. A: _____ _____ _____ OK if I didn't turn in my homework today?

   B: _____, no _____. Just turn it in tomorrow.

C On a separate piece of paper, write the opposite responses to each question in **B**.

LESSON B

Verb + Infinitive vs. Verb + Gerund	
I **need** <u>to buy</u> a new phone.	Certain verbs can be followed by an <u>infinitive</u> (*to* + verb).
I **avoid** <u>talking</u> on the phone when I'm driving.	Other verbs can be followed by a <u>gerund</u> (verb + *-ing*).
I **tried** <u>to call</u> / <u>calling</u> you earlier.	Some verbs can be followed by an infinitive or a gerund.

Verbs followed by an infinitive		Verbs followed by a gerund		Verbs followed by an infinitive or a gerund	
agree	need	appreciate	finish	begin	love
choose	plan	avoid	imagine	can't stand	prefer
decide	seem	dislike	keep	hate	start
hope	want	enjoy	(not) mind	like	try
learn	would like	feel like	suggest		

A Underline the gerund or the infinitive in each sentence. Then check (✓) the correct sentences. Change the incorrect sentences.

1. ☐ I learned to speak Spanish in high school.
2. ☐ I avoid to call people on the phone.
3. ☐ I began to raise my voice.
4. ☐ I enjoy to play games on my phone.
5. ☐ I agreed turning down the music on my phone.
6. ☐ I prefer to respond to texts quickly.
7. ☐ I finished to do my homework and then I called a friend.
8. ☐ I tried texting you twice but you didn't reply.

B Complete each question with the infinitive or gerund form of the word in parentheses. Sometimes both forms are possible.

1. What do you need (do) _____*to do*_____ this weekend?
2. Who's someone you'd like (meet) _____?
3. What's something you can't stand (do) _____?
4. When did you start (learn) _____ English?
5. What TV shows do you enjoy (watch) _____?

C Now answer the questions in **B**. Use complete sentences.

Example: *I love hanging out with my friends.*

1. _____
2. _____
3. _____
4. _____
5. _____

NOTES

NOTES

NOTES

NOTES

NOTES

NOTES

NOTES